LAOS

About the Book and Author

Theravada Buddhists in the lowlands and animists in the mountains, the people of Laos have wanted nothing more than to live at peace. Unfortunately, their country's location between two more powerful neighbors, Vietnam and Thailand, has made it the victim of invasion and domination since the fifteenth century. In this analytic introduction to Laos, Arthur Dommen traces first the country's history and culture up to its independence from France in 1954. He then examines the more recent events that have brought Laos to its current status in Asia: its three successive and short-lived attempts to form coalition governments; the big-power efforts, ending in failure, to win the neutralization of Laos; the construction by the North Vietnamese of what later became the Ho Chi Minh Trail; and the process by which the U.S. military became increasingly and painfully involved in Laos on the ground and in the air. Looking at the country's present political system, its economy, society, culture, and its international relations, Dr. Dommen assesses the aftermath of the 1975 Communist takeover of Laos and the consequent establishment of a people's democracy. The new regime has brought a relative peace to Laos; yet many have preferred flight to the "re-education" camps; and internal resistance (abetted by China) to Vietnamese domination continues to make peace illusory. Laos's rulers may, suggests Dr. Dommen, come to seek a measure of independence from Hanoi's dictates.

Arthur J. Dommen is an agricultural economist with the Africa and Middle East Branch, International Economics Division, Economic Research Service, U.S. Department of Agriculture. He was formerly bureau chief for the *Los Angeles Times* in Tokyo, New Delhi, and Saigon and for United Press International in Saigon and Hong Kong, as well as a Paris correspondent covering the Vietnam negotiations in 1968 and 1969.

LAOS

Keystone
of Indochina

Arthur J. Dommen

Westview Press / Boulder and London

EB

Profiles/Nations of Contemporary Asia

The cover photo, by Peter Robinson, is a detail of the wood carved door, Wat Pa Khe, Luang Prabang.

Copyright © 1985 by Westview Press, Inc.

Published in 1985 in the United States of America by Westview Press, Inc.; Frederick A. Praeger, Publisher; 5500 Central Avenue, Boulder, Colorado 80301

Library of Congress Cataloging in Publication Data
Dommen, Arthur J.
    Laos: Keystone of Indochina.
    (Westview profiles. Nations of contemporary Asia)
    Bibliography: p.
    Includes index.
    1. Laos. I. Title. II. Series.
DS555.3.D65 1985   959.4′04   85-5307
ISBN 0-86531-771-2

Printed and bound in the United States of America

10   9   8   7   6   5   4   3   2   1

12-2-85

To my parents

Contents

Illustrations

Preface

When I first started writing about the post-1954 conflict in Laos in the mid-1960s, although I talked to a great many reliable witnesses and participants in historical events, including Vietnamese, and read the first-hand accounts of the Lao, the French, and others, I had no very definite idea of the nature of Hanoi's "grand design" for the kingdom of the Million Elephants. The Vietnamese Communists, it seemed clear, had made use of the Vietnamese community in Laos (and in Thailand) to organize and lead the resistance against the returning French after World War II. The resistance in Laos was an extension of the Vietnamese Communists' own revolution, and when it turned against the Vientiane government as its enemy, it became totally dependent on the Vietnamese for sanctuary, leadership, and military wherewithal, which included "volunteers."

Only when I began to read the history of the Indochinese Communist party, however, was the true nature of the umbilical cord linking the two revolutions revealed, and it provided an explanation for much that was happening. At the same time, it cast a spotlight on what the future likely held: an interesting case of traveling backward in time to see more clearly forward.

Aside from participants in events, those who have been kind enough to give me the benefit of their knowledge, when asked about particular points in conversations or correspondence, include Professor Kanji Akagi, Amphay Doré, Arnold

R. Isaacs, Phouratsamy Naughton, Roy Pepper, Douglas Pike, Martin Stuart-Fox, Professor O. W. Wolters, and Professor David K. Wyatt. They are in no way responsible for my interpretations.

The spelling of place names in this book generally conforms to that used in the map by Eugene M. Scheel and Victor J. Kelley, in Peter T. White, "Report on Laos," *National Geographic Magazine* 120, no. 2 (August 1961):250–251.

I am grateful to Mervyn W. Adams Seldon and to my editors at Westview Press, Libby Barstow and Pat Peterson, for their careful editing of the manuscript. Also to my wife, Loan, for her ever-present support.

Arthur J. Dommen
Bethesda, Maryland

MAP 1   Laos: Physical Setting

1

Land and People

GEOGRAPHICAL SETTING

Like a wedge at the summit of an arch, Laos occupies a key position on the map of Indochina. From Burma and Thailand on the west to Vietnam on the east, with its foundations in the Malay peninsula and the Indonesian archipelago, the arch supports the weight of China and the mass of Central Asia, another world—an image evocative, perhaps, of an age of monument building long past. But like the keystone of an arch, Laos has the dual function of holding apart the other, larger stones so they do not tumble and fall and of tying all together so the structure thus created is solid. Throughout its history, Laos has had this dual role.

Laos is a landlocked country on the Indochinese Peninsula. The southern half of the country lies between the Mekong River on the west and the Annamite Chain on the east. In the north, the country is not encapsulated between well-defined geophysical features but constitutes part of the extremely mountainous land form that extends all the way from southern China across to northern Thailand and Burma and through which the Mekong River has cut its path. Laos's total area is approximately 91,000 square miles (235,690 square kilometers).

Laos's Indochinese neighbors are Vietnam to the east, with which it shares a 1,324-mile-long (2,131-kilometer-long) border; Cambodia to the south; and Thailand to the west. To the north, Laos shares common borders with Burma and China. Laos, Vietnam, and Cambodia formed French Indo-

1

china, and despite official insistence on the Lao language, French remains the lingua franca of the region.

The country's relief is highly complex; mountains and hills predominate. Although elevations generally decrease from east to west and from north to south, numerous plateaus and escarpments form distinct landscape features. Much of the land is steeply sloped to narrow river bottoms in which cultivation is possible. The mountains are densely forested for the most part, but in some areas, in the south particularly, sparse glade forest and savanna prevail. Along the Mekong River lie the country's only extensive alluvial plains, formed by the great river and its tributaries. In the north lies the Plain of Jars, a wide area of rolling hills covered by grass and tree groves. In the south, the Bolovens Plateau dominates the landscape before the succession of ridge lines rises to the crest of the Annamite Chain.

The climate of Laos is highly seasonal. A southwest monsoon prevails from May until September, bringing moisture up from the Gulf of Thailand that falls as torrential rain in spots along the western slopes of the Annamite Chain. A dry season under the influence of the northeast monsoon begins in October and lasts until April. The first rains come as thunderstorms. As the rainy season progresses, rain falls more evenly and for more extended periods, with a peak in July and August. During the dry season the rainfall slackens and then ceases altogether so that some months have no rains at all. The driest months—December, January, and February— are also the coldest. Thereafter the temperature begins to rise, reaching its maximum at the very end of the dry season.

Water flow of the rivers in the country follows a pattern dictated by this rainfall regime. The Mekong, entering Laos from the high Tibetan plateau in China, passes through deep gorges and enters a true plain for the first time in the Vientiane region. Farther south, it passes through narrow defiles before entering the Cambodian plain. Numerous rocky outcroppings and sand banks make the river virtually useless for navigation in Laos except by small boats. The same may be said of its major tributaries, which are from north to south the Nam Tha, the Nam Beng, the Nam Hou, the Nam Soung, the Nam

Landscape near Vang Vieng. (Photo in author's collection)

Khan (at Luang Prabang), the Nam Lik, the Nam Ngum (which flows onto the plain of Vientiane), the Nam Sane, the Nam Ca Dinh, the Se Bang Fai, the Se Bang Hieng, the Se Done, and the Se Kong (which enters the Mekong in Cambodia) (see Map 1).

Laos has five major roads. Route 13 connects the former royal capital of Luang Prabang with the administrative capital of Vientiane and then follows the left bank of the Mekong around to Paksane and south to Thakhek, Savannakhet, Pakse, and to the Cambodian border in the vicinity of the falls at Khong Island. Route 7 crosses the Barthélémy Pass east of the Plain of Jars and connects with Route 13 at Sala Phou Khoun. The other main roads are Route 8 from the Keo Neua Pass to Thakhek; Route 12 from the Mu Gia Pass to Na Phao; and Route 9 from the Lao Bao Pass to Savannakhet.

ETHNOGRAPHY

The crest of the Annamite Chain marks the dividing line between Asia's two most important cultures, the Indian and the Chinese. In our times, the Indianized peoples of Southeast Asia live to the west of this line, whereas the Sinicized people, namely the Vietnamese, live to its east.[1] Fearing the mountains, inhospitable and insalubrious, the peoples on either side of this cultural divide have historically occupied the plains, more suitable for lowland, irrigated paddy cultivation. This pattern is followed by the Lao[2] as well as the Thai and the Khmer on the west and the Vietnamese on the east.

On either side of the dividing line, the high mountain country has been peopled by minorities, either the aboriginal inhabitants of Indochina or later migrants. For their own security or livelihood, these peoples settled in scattered villages in forest clearings, cultivating by the ancient method of slash-and-burn on the mountain slopes. This ethnographic feature has had an important political consequence: When modern rulers and colonial administrators have had to draw the boundary between the states centering on the lowland peoples to the west and to the east of the divide, they naturally have chosen the divide along the Annamite Chain. But the political boundary they have created cuts through the lands of eth-nographically similar peoples, who thus find themselves be-longing to different nations, and who can be enlisted by one to act as its agents in the other.

The largest single group in Laos, the Lao Loum, or lowland Lao, number about 1.7 million.[3] They are Theravada Buddhists (Buddhists of the Little Vehicle), as are the Thai and other Indianized peoples of Southeast Asia. The Buddhist priesthood, or Sangha, enjoys great respect among the Lao and plays an important role in Lao society. The Lao of the left bank of the Mekong are ethnically identical with the Lao of the right bank, who live in present-day northeast Thailand (the provinces of Udorn, Sakhorn Nakhon, Ubon, and so on).

Who are the minority peoples who constitute, in the case of Laos, approximately one-half the population of the country? Although they differ considerably in language, social customs, and history, they have the common characteristic that they are animists, as opposed to the lowland Lao who are Theravada Buddhists.[4] The largest minority group of

Hmong girls. (Photo in author's collection)

people, numbering about nine hundred thousand in January 1980, are the Lao Theung (Lao of the mountainsides). These include the large group of people believed to be descendants of the aboriginal inhabitants of Laos. According to a Lao legend, these people sprang from one of three giant gourds, and when the Lao moved to occupy the lowlands, they forced the retreat of these Kha, or slaves, into the mountains. Today the Lao Theung live in wood longhouses on piles and cultivate upland rice, maize, tobacco, and cotton. They are the principal minority of southern Laos.

The Lao T'ai consist of a number of tribes who migrated into Laos over an extended period and who all speak the same basic language. They are said to number about five hundred thousand. Their houses are typically built on wooden pilings with bamboo walls and thatched roofs. The areas under their houses are used as stables and as working places for weaving cloth. The Lao T'ai are wet rice cultivators. The basic religion of the T'ai is animism. Their spirits, or genies, are called *phi,* and everything that occurs in everyday life, particularly misfortune, is attributed to them. They are omnipresent, and every village has a sacred grove where the *phi* live.

✶✶✶ The next most numerous minority group is the Lao Soung (Lao of the mountaintops), numbering some four hundred and fifty thousand. They are peoples who migrated from southern China relatively recently and include the Hmong (known also as Meo or Miao) and the Yao (or Man). The Hmong, until their decimation in the war and at the hands of Laos's new rulers and their mass exodus to the United States and other countries, were known as the warrior race of Laos, akin to the Gurkhas of Nepal. They build their houses on the ground and their villages on the mountain tops. Indefatigable walkers and horsemen, they are hunters and cultivators of maize, vegetables, and the opium poppy. Their language is of the Tibeto-Burman group. The Hmong celebrate several feasts associated with forest spirits and cultivation. One of these is held at the new year; another at the opening of the planting season, when sacrifices are made to the spirit of the mountain who protects the harvest; and a third at harvest time. Funerals are occasions for feasting as well. The Yao, like the Hmong, are practitioners of shifting cultivation. Their religion is a mixture of animistic belief in spirits, the cult of the ancestors, and belief in survival of souls. Their priests play an important role in social organization.

The other important minorities of Laos are the Vietnamese and the Chinese. Vietnamese settlement in Laos, first encouraged by the French and then by the Hanoi government, was reported to have reached a total of four hundred thousand persons in early 1985.[5] About twenty thousand people of Chinese origin live in Laos, mainly in the towns.

NOTES

1. The Vietnamese and Chinese communities in countries like Laos, Cambodia, and Thailand are exceptions to this generalization.

2. Following customary usage, the term *Lao* will be used in this book to refer to the lowland Lao and the term *Laotian* to refer to the inhabitants of the state or country of Laos.

3. The population figures given here are estimates. The first census in Laos's modern history took place in March 1985.

4. See Chapter 9 for additional information on religion.

5. Uthit Pasakhom, "Beyond a Soviet-Vietnamese Condominium: The Case of Laos," *Indochina Report* (Singapore), January–March 1985, p. 7. This figure does not include the personnel of the Vietnamese army stationed in Laos.

2

The Precolonial Period (to 1893)

Laos has been inhabited by human beings since well before the beginning of its recorded history, which spans more than six centuries. On the basis of human remains and artifacts, the great French classical scholar George Coedès affirmed that the oldest human inhabitants of Southeast Asia probably lived in the Phou Loi massif north of the Plain of Jars. This must have been at a time when the cultivation of paddy rice by controlled flooding was as yet unknown. For such hunters and gatherers, the mountains afforded greater security than the plains. Much later, when humans had learned the arts of herding and cultivation, the more than one hundred stone jars that gave their name to the plain were carved and used, most probably as funerary urns, by people whose identity remains uncertain.

EARLY HISTORY

In the first century A.D., Chinese writings for the first time supplement the archaeological record for our knowledge of mainland Southeast Asia. The Chinese accounts speak of "states," based on the notion that centralized administration would be necessary then to account for the flourishing trade. But we should think more properly perhaps of these as centers of kingly power extending outward, waxing and waning in accordance with the vigor and credibility of the ruler, and occasionally overlapping with that of a neighbor. All this would have been in the context of vast and as yet sparsely populated forests and swamplands, for the inhabitants of the mountainous areas remained beyond the pale.

Notable among such centers of power were Funan (so called by the Chinese), with its capital Vidhayapura on the lower Mekong River, and Champa, a collection of principalities stretching along the coast but extending inland to encompass southern Laos, as the name Champassak attests. Both had been founded by colonists from India, around the beginning of the Christian era, who impressed on them the Indian conception of royalty, Hinduist cults, and the use of the Sanskrit language. Finally, centered on the Red River delta was the embryo of the future state of Vietnam, then under Chinese rule (Map 2a).

Sometime in the second half of the fifth century, however, a vassal of Funan named Shreshthavarman was victorious over the Chams of Champassak and founded a city at the foot of a hillside sanctuary, Wat Phou, which had long been the site of a linga cult of a type closely associated with the Indianized monarchies of ancient Indochina. The city was named Shreshthapura (Map 2b). These events in an obscure corner of Indochina had enormous political consequences: A princess of the maternal line of Shreshthavarman, Kambu-jarajalakshmi (whose name means "the fortune of the Kam-bujan kings"), transmitted the heritage of Shreshthavarman to her spouse Bhavavarman, who in turn became one of the founders of the first identifiable Khmer state, Kambuja-desa. Some two hundred years later, Angkor became the capital of this vast empire, the successor of Funan, with a territory that included most of Laos (Map 2c). The Chinese called the empire Chen-la.

Meanwhile, people coming from another cultural center in the lower Menam valley had introduced Theravada Buddhism[1] to the inhabitants of the upper Mekong valley. This change had far-reaching effects because Theravada Buddhism had great mass appeal, unlike Hinduism, in which rituals were often confined to the ruling elite. The origin of the introduction, judging by stone images of Buddha and carved Mon inscriptions found in the Nam Ngum valley, was

11

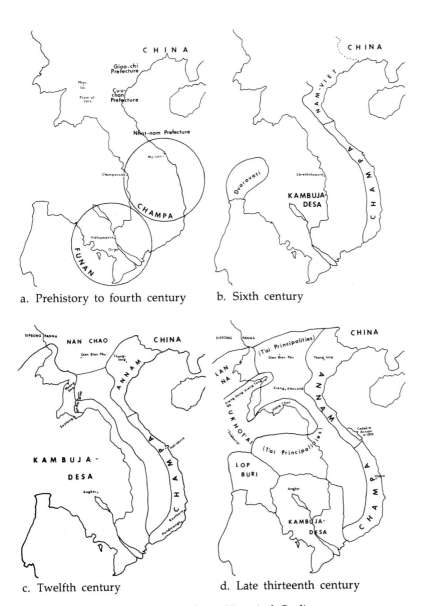

a. Prehistory to fourth century   b. Sixth century

c. Twelfth century   d. Late thirteenth century

MAP 2   Indochina: Historical Outline

the kingdom of Dvaravati (Map 2b), which by the early eighth century had spawned outposts, probably along trade routes, on the upper Menam. The inhabitants of Dvaravati were ethnically related to the aboriginal inhabitants of central Laos, from whom they were geographically separated by only a thin band of easily crossed territory, and they were fervent Buddhists.

Between the sixth and thirteenth centuries, Indochina saw the southward migration from China of the T'ai peoples, a new element in the region. They intermarried freely with the indigenous inhabitants, and the descendants of these newcomers include the lowland Lao of today. Others among these migrants were the settlers in the Menam valley whom the Khmer called the Syam; the Lu, who settled in Nam Tha and Phong Saly; the T'ai N'ua, who settled much of northern Laos and in Sayaboury; the T'ai Deng (Red T'ai), in Sam Neua; the T'ai Dam (Black T'ai), south of the Plain of Jars; and the T'ai Khao (White T'ai), in Phong Saly. At various points during their long migration, the T'ai formed princi-palities of their own, and in Chinese and Vietnamese writings about these principalities we first see the word *Lao* used: *Ngai Lao* in the former and *Ai Lao* in the latter.[2]

The T'ai who moved down the river valleys and founded the first Lao principality at Muong Swa (the Mon-Khmer name for Luang Prabang) apparently at first kept close relations with Kambuja-desa, the preeminent but waning power in the region. The reign name of Muong Swa's family was Khun, and its origin coincides with a Lao legend explaining the creation of the world. In their uncivilized state, the people lived by hunting and fishing. Irritated by their bestial behavior, the celestial spirit caused a deluge on earth, which the three earthly chiefs, named Khun, survived by building an ark. Afterward, the celestial spirit forgave them and sent them back to earth with the present of a water buffalo, with which the three Khuns began to make paddy fields. But the buffalo died, and out of its nostrils grew three giant gourds. One of the Khuns took a red-hot iron and pierced a gourd and people emerged. He cut the others with a pair of scissors, and more people emerged. The first of these groups, blackened with soot, was the Kha. Out of the other two gourds emerged the Lao and the Lao aristocracy.

Because of the difficulties the three Khuns had in organizing this multitude, the celestial spirit sent down to earth his son, Khun Borom, who arrived riding an elephant with crossed tusks. (Historically, Khun Borom may have been the founder of an eighth-century principality in the area of Dien Bien Phu, which was part of the T'ai kingdom of Nanchao.) While Khun Borom was instructing the people in the arts of civilization, a giant liana grew up and obscured the sky so that the earth became cold. An old couple from Khun Borom's cortege gained immortality by cutting down this liana, which fell after three months and three days of chopping, killing them both. Khun Borom instructed his seven sons to colonize seven territories. Muong Swa went to a son named Khun Lo.

Khun became an honorary title used by Khun Lo's thirteen successors. After them, the title of Muong Swa's rulers became Thao (meaning "prince") and finally Panya (meaning "he who upholds"). The first Panya, Langthirat, incurred the displeasure of his people and was placed in a cage near the mouth of the Nam Hou. His son, Panya Kamphong, banished his own son, Phi Fa, for having seduced one of Panya Kamphong's wives. Phi Fa then went into exile at Angkor, taking with him his young son Fa Ngum (whose birth in 1316 is perhaps the first event fixed in Lao history).

During the thirteenth century, political conditions in Indochina had changed drastically. The southward movement of the T'ai had been greatly accelerated by the Mongol Kublai Khan's conquest of Nanchao. In 1238, two Syam chiefs had seized power from the Khmer commander at Sukhot'ai, meaning that the northwest frontier of Kambuja-desa was crumbling. By the end of the thirteenth century, under the leadership of a powerful king, Rama Kamheng, Sukhot'ai had been expanded eastward to gain suzerainty over Muong Swa. Rama Kamheng's son was bold enough to use Muong Swa to stage attacks against Vietnam—these attacks were very probably the first instances of direct conflict between the Syam and the Vietnamese. Farther down the Mekong, a series of lesser

T'ai chiefs replaced centralized Khmer control over the remainder of Laos (Map 2d).

The arrival at his court, therefore, of two exiled members
of the ruling family of Muong Swa provided the Kambujan
king, Jayavarman Paramesvara, with a heaven-sent opportunity. The young Fa Ngum was brought up at the court
and at the age of sixteen married one of the king's daughters.
When the time came, Jayavarman, seeing the power of Sukhot'ai decline suddenly, dispatched Fa Ngum and his father
at the head of an army of ten thousand Khmer.

THE KINGDOM OF LAN XANG

After defeating the chief of Champassak and putting to
flight that of Khammouane, Fa Ngum proceeded to Xieng
Khouang, which he captured and whose chief, the descendant
of another of Khun Borom's sons, he ordered executed. He
placed on the throne another ruler, who became his vassal.
He negotiated a border treaty with the ruler of neighboring
Vietnam, which established the watershed between the Mekong and the Gulf of Tonkin. He then proceeded to lay seige
to Xieng Dong Xieng Tong, the T'ai name for Muong Swa,
and (his father having died) acceded to the throne in place
of his grandfather, who committed suicide in shame.

Fa Ngum consolidated his realm by further military
expeditions to the north and east. His most dramatic campaign
was against Vieng Chan to the south, which he captured by
a ruse. In 1353, Fa Ngum's coronation took place. The new
kingdom (Map 3a) was called Lan Xang—Kingdom of the
Million Elephants. Later, Fa Ngum extended his domains as
far as Tchepone in the east. To the south, he invaded the
Korat Plateau and captured Roi Et. The Syam had founded
a new capital at Ayuthia in 1350. The king of Ayuthia, instead
of attempting to enforce his claims to the region as the
successor of the king of Sukhot'ai, made peace with Fa Ngum
and sent him tribute and one of his daughters.

In internal affairs, Fa Ngum reformed and reinvigorated
Buddhism, which had apparently become corrupted; made
Theravada Buddhism the state religion; and encouraged the

15

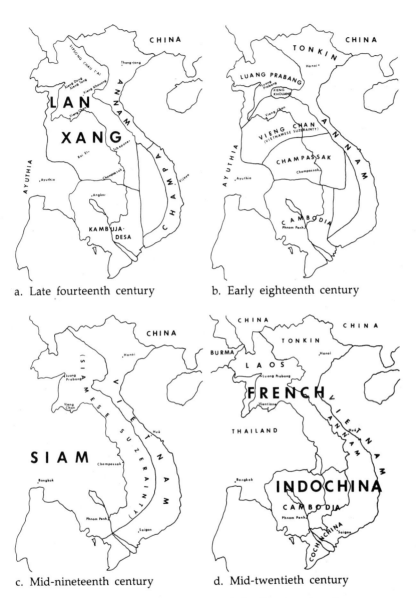

a. Late fourteenth century

b. Early eighteenth century

c. Mid-nineteenth century

d. Mid-twentieth century

MAP 3 Indochina: Historical Outline (continued)

Statues of Buddha, Wat May, Luang Prabang. The standing statue is the Prabang. (Photo in author's collection)

arts. He sent his old Khmer religious teacher to lead a religious and artistic mission to Angkor. This mission brought back sacred texts and a statue of the standing Buddha endowed with magical powers—the Prabang—that had been sent to Angkor five hundred years before from Ceylon. The statue was preserved in a special pagoda in the town.

Fa Ngum's military successes seem to have turned his head. His ministers finally drove him into exile in 1373, and he died shortly thereafter. He was succeeded by his son Oun Hueun, who is known by the name Panya Sam Sen T'ai, or King of the Three Hundred Thousand T'ai, after the census of males completed in 1376. His reign (1373–1416) was generally a peaceful one marked by the building of many pagodas (*wats*). He had taken the precaution of marrying a princess of Ayuthia, and his administration bore the stamp of Siamese methods.

Peace did not last, however, During the reign of Lan Kham Deng (1416–1428), an army of thirty thousand warriors and one hundred elephants sent in aid of Emperor Le Loi of Vietnam committed treason and joined the Chinese it was meant to fight. The exasperated Vietnamese succeeded in driving the army back into Lan Xang, but the experience sowed the seeds of future conflict. It was just as well for Lan Xang that the Vietnamese were occupied during those years with the final reduction of Champa, which succumbed in 1471, because its throne was the object of family intrigues stirred up by Sam Sen T'ai's eldest daughter, Nang Keo Pimpa. Seven kings succeeded each other in the period 1428–1438; all were her lovers, and she had each one killed in turn. Not content with intriguing, she finally took the throne herself and was executed after barely four months.

In 1478, after long preparation the Vietnamese attacked, passing through Xieng Khouang and capturing Xieng Dong Xieng Tong after a bitter fight. The king, Sai Tiakaphat (reign 1438–1479), fled downriver. Victory soon turned to defeat for the invaders, however, as the king's son, Prince Theng Kham, rallied the Lao and pushed the Vietnamese out of the kingdom. The father then vacated the throne in favor of his son, who took the reign name Souvanna Palang (1479–1486).

A period of peace and rebuilding followed, marked by closer relations with Ayuthia. In 1507, another great king acceded to the throne in the midst of a thunderstorm, whence his reign name of Visoun (meaning "Lightning Bolt"). Visoun's son, Potisarat (reign 1520–1547), justified his name (meaning, "future Buddha") by encouraging Buddhism and proscribing, in an edict of 1527, the animist sacrifices to the spirits of the locality. Potisarat also won a decisive victory over a Siamese army sent to besiege Vieng Chan in 1536. Under his son Sai Setthathirath (reign 1548–1571), however, relations with Ayuthia improved to such an extent that a treaty of friendship was concluded in 1560, commemorated by an inscription defining the border as the watershed between the Nan and the Mekong. Sai Setthathirath even moved the capital to Vieng Chan, possibly for better communications with Ayuthia, but more likely because the Burmese were beginning to make menacing noises in the west. During his reign Xieng Dong Xieng Tong was renamed Luang Prabang in honor of the Prabang, and Vieng Chan was enriched with monuments and pagodas.

A period of troubles followed, punctuated by numerous succession disputes and intervention in the affairs of Lan Xang by both the Siamese and the Burmese. These troubles were followed by a peaceful and constructive reign, that of Souligna Vongsa (1637–1694), the Sun King of Laos, a contemporary of Louis XIV of France. Backed by a strong army, he maintained peace with his neighbors and achieved much, including a further identification of the kingdom's borders. Vieng Chan was a proud city and Souligna Vongsa a stern king who, according to accounts by Dutch traders and Portuguese missionaries, acknowledged no superior. Nevertheless, in his determination to see justice applied, he made a fatal mistake: He refused to stay the execution of his only son, who had been found guilty of adultery, and thereby set the stage for the most serious succession crisis up to then.

THE THREE KINGDOMS

For 350 years the territories unified by Fa Ngum constituted a powerful kingdom in Indochina, a state in the true sense of the term, delineated by borders clearly defined and consecrated by treaty. Although the ruling monarchy was occasionally racked by internal disputes about the interpretation of its rules of succession, it claimed authority over a population composed of diverse ethnic groups and religions. The monarchy may have been a feudal one, with all the pejorative meaning we attach to the term today, but Lao historians see in the nomenclature in use at the time a positive proof of the existence of a distinct Lao race (*sua sat Lao*), a Lao nation (*sat Lao*), a Lao country (*muong Lao*), and a Lao state (*pathet Lao*). In view of these facts, we may safely reject the notion, fashionable among apologists for a colonial enterprise of a later day, that Laos was a creation of French colonial policy and administration.

Souligna Vongsa's death in 1694 left two grandsons, Kitsarat and Inthathom, both minors, as the heirs to the throne. It is not known whether the rules of succession laid down by Fa Ngum provided for cases of regency; in any event, the chief minister proclaimed himself king. Six years later, he was overthrown by a provincial governor and Kitsarat and Inthathom fled to Luang Prabang. Souligna Vongsa had a nephew who had been living all this while at the court of Annam. Known as Sai Ong Hue, he had been agitating since 1696 for Vietnamese help in invading Lan Xang, and his offer of suzerainty in exchange for this help persuaded the Nguyen emperor, who in any case was pursuing a policy of territorial aggrandizement to the south. He provided Sai Ong Hue with Vietnamese soldiers, enabling this pretender to capture Vieng Chan in 1700 and put to death the usurper.

Sai Ong Hue dispatched his half brother to take possession of Luang Prabang, forcing Kitsarat and Inthathom to seek safety in the Sipsong Panna, the country around Muong Sing, where a friendly cousin ruled. The latter raised an army on their behalf, and in 1707 they recaptured Luang Prabang, but not before the Prabang, the palladium of the kingdom, had been carried off to Vieng Chan. Kitsarat proclaimed himself king and sent an ultimatum to Sai Ong Hue that he should henceforth consider the provinces north of the Thuong River as constituting a kingdom outside his sovereignty. The effect of this was to cut Lan Xang in two: a kingdom of Vieng Chan comprising all middle and southern Laos as far west as the watershed of the Menam owing suzerainty to the Vietnamese, and a kingdom of Luang Prabang maintaining a precarious independence.

In Champassak another nephew of Souligna Vongsa, Soi Sisamout, seceded from Vieng Chan and reigned from 1713 onward, maintaining good relations with the Siamese and the Khmer. Lan Xang was now divided into three parts (Map 3b), each entertaining relations of vassalage not unlike the feudal kingdoms of medieval France. These relations, however, were to be the source of much conflict.

BETWEEN SIAM AND ANNAM

In Vieng Chan, Sai Ong Hue was succeeded peacefully by his son, Ong Long (reign 1735–1760), whose reign saw great convulsions in Siam and Burma. Ong Long avoided occupation of his kingdom by the expanding Burmese by assisting them in their invasion of Luang Prabang. In Xieng Khouang, Ong Long compelled the ruler to pay tribute, but again only at the price of yet another Vietnamese intervention in the affairs of that sensitive border principality.

A Burmese army intervened again in 1771 on the side of Vieng Chan to relieve a two-month-long siege of Vieng Chan by an army from Luang Prabang. In 1778 the Siamese, who were determined to secure their northern flank against the Burmese, sent an expedition against Vieng Chan, allied with the Burmese (there was apparently no lack of pretexts), sacking the city, and carrying off to Bangkok the Prabang as well as all the members of the royal family. Not until three years later when the Siamese ended their military rule over Vieng Chan and enthroned Chao Nanthasen (reign 1781–1792) was the Prabang returned. Henceforth Vieng Chan had to acknowledge Siamese suzerainty. By this time, Champassak had done the same.

In 1791, Nanthasen, taking advantge of a succession struggle in Luang Prabang, captured it and annexed the Hua Phan (Sam Neua). As the aged king of Luang Prabang, Inthathom, had signed a treaty of alliance with Siam in 1774, Nanthasen's action provoked Siamese displeasure, and he was replaced as king by his younger brother, Chao In (reign 1792–

1805), whose yet younger brother and viceroy (*oupahat*) was to become the last king of Vieng Chan, Chao Anou.

Acknowledging Siamese suzerainty, however, did not prevent Vieng Chan from continuing close relations with Annam. Some princely states under Vieng Chan's hegemony, such as Xieng Khouang, had long been paying tribute both to Vieng Chan and Annam, and this attention to the east increased as the power of Annam grew. Forces from Vieng Chan cooperated with Annamese Emperor Gia Long against the Tay-son rebellion in Annam, and in 1798 Vietnamese officers came to Vieng Chan to aid its forces against rebel bands. Vieng Chan sent tribute missions to Gia Long in 1801 and 1802, and on the latter's accession to the throne in 1804 formally acknowledged its status of vassal; the emperor returned the acknowledgment, agreed to a triennial tribute, and sent the tributary mission home loaded with presents. In this period of Siamese intervention in the territories to the east, it was only a matter of time before the interests of Siam and Annam collided.

Chao Anou, while still viceroy of Vieng Chan, started out by earning the reputation in Siamese eyes of being a loyal servant. He commanded Lao contingents fighting at the side of the Siamese army in 1795, 1798, 1799, and 1803. He distinguished himself in these campaigns, which were mainly against the Burmese, and was twice commended by King Rama I of Siam. Events soon afforded him the opportunity he had been waiting for to prepare for a confrontation with Siam.

In 1819, a revolt broke out among the Kha of Champassak, led by a renegade monk named Sa, who claimed magical powers, which he demonstrated by using a mirror to create fire. Sa gathered a large number of followers and marched on Champassak. The ruler allowed his city to be overrun and fled across the Mekong. The Siamese put down the rebellion but did not capture Sa, who was captured by a force from Vieng Chan led by Chao Anou's son, Nho. Chao Anou was then able to prevail on the Siamese king to enthrone Nho as king of Champassak, despite Siamese misgivings about adding to the strength of the ruler of Vieng Chan.

In January 1827, Chao Anou and Chao Nho launched a foolhardy enterprise by marching their troops on Bangkok. They had lined up assurances of support from Annam if needed, or so they believed, and had tried to keep Luang Prabang at least neutral by circulating rumors that a British naval force was preparing an attack against Bangkok. Only when they reached Saraburi, three days' march from Bangkok, did they meet the Siamese army, which scattered and expelled the Lao forces.

The Siamese, who by now were embarked on a policy of vigorous presence in the Lao territories, reacted to this impudent and imprudent challenge by sacking Vieng Chan, as the Romans had destroyed Carthage after the Second Punic War. Intent on preventing a resurgence of Lao power, they forced the Lao population to resettle on the right bank of the Mekong. The territories of the defunct kingdom of Vieng Chan were placed under direct Siamese provincial administration, where they remained for the next sixty-six years (Map 3c). By fragmenting the former kingdom of Lan Xang still further, leaving only a weakly independent Luang Prabang, the Siamese were sowing the seeds of trouble for themselves, as David Wyatt has pointed out.

After a short-lived attempt to reoccupy Vieng Chan with the help of Vietnamese soldiers, Chao Anou fled to Xieng Khouang, where the ruler Chao Noi handed him over to the Siamese. He died in Bangkok in 1835. The Vietnamese Emperor Minh Mang had Chao Noi executed in Hué and annexed Xieng Khouang to Annam in 1832 as the prefecture of Tran Ninh.

During Chao Anou's disastrous confrontation with the Siamese, the King of Luang Prabang, Manta Tourat (reign 1817–1836), had maintained his neutrality. Siamese influence at the court of Luang Prabang, we may deduce, was very strong. As they had done in Vieng Chan, the Siamese set up a younger brother of the king, Oun Keo, as viceroy. Although Manta Tourat owed allegiance to Siam, he nevertheless sent missions to Hué in 1831 and 1833, offering homage and the traditional tribute of gold and silver. Minh Mang was not anxious to provoke the Siamese, however, and he therefore pigeonholed the offers. After Manta Tourat's death, his letters proved a godsend to the agents of a newly arrived power on the scene—the French—who were as much interested in the territories on the left bank of the Mekong as were the Siamese.

NOTES

1. For a description of Theravada Buddhism, see Chapter 9.
2. Meaning "first (elder) of the Lao."

3

The Colonial Period and the First Geneva Conference (1893–1954)

In 1859, the government of Napoleon III intervened directly in Vietnam, launching France's colonial enterprise in Indochina. Four years later, the French imposed their protectorate on Cambodia. The first French person to penetrate into Laos, however, was neither a soldier nor an administrator, but a naturalist. He was Henri Mouhot, who had earlier discovered the ruins of Angkor in the Cambodian rain forest. Mouhot had died of malaria on the banks of the Nam Khan not far from Luang Prabang in 1861 during the reign of Tiantha Koumane (1851–1872), to whom King Mongkut of Siam had restored the famous Prabang.

Mouhot was followed by explorers seeking a river road to China. But the times were unfavorable for developing trade with China, even if the Mekong had proved navigable. The Taiping rebellion had been crushed, and northern Indochina was soon flooded with refugees, called Ho by the T'ai. The ravages of these lawless bands, who went by the names of Black Flags, Yellow Flags, and so on, put an end to the nearly one hundred years of peace that Luang Prabang had enjoyed under Siamese suzerainty.

A first round of skirmishes between the Siamese and the Ho, initiated in response to an appeal for help from King Oun Kham (reign 1872–1887), ended inconclusively with the withdrawal of the Ho to their bases in Xieng Khouang. An attempt to storm these bases in 1883 failed, and so in 1885, a year after France had won the right to place its residents over the mandarin administrators of Annam and Tonkin, the Siamese dispatched a stronger force to occupy the whole country to the north and east of Luang Prabang right up to the basin of the Black River. The commander of this force appointed two commissioners (*kha luang*) to oversee affairs at the side of Oun Kham.

THE EVICTION OF SIAM

Thereupon the Quai d'Orsay sent a warning note to Bangkok and invited the court of Annam to formulate its claims in the area. A provisional agreement was concluded on May 7, 1886, sanctioning the establishment of a French vice-consulate at Luang Prabang. Although the man chosen for this post, Auguste Pavie of Dinan in Brittany, appeared to have few resources at his disposal, he more than made up for this lack by ingenuity and dedication to his multiple responsibilities.

The Siamese commissioners succeeded at first in frustrating Pavie's attempts to make contact with the septuagenarian Oun Kham. Moreover, the Siamese commander returned with the news that the whole country had been cleared of the invaders and produced a map showing the territories owing allegiance to the King. Pavie thereupon busied himself with preparations for a mission he had been given to explore a practicable route between the Mekong and Tonkin. Warned by the local inhabitants of the country he was passing through of an impending attack on the capital, Pavie retraced his steps to Luang Prabang, where he found that the overconfident Siamese commander, convinced that the invaders would not attack during the rainy season, had already departed for Bangkok with the bulk of his army, the chief commissioner, a number of hostages, and the eldest son of the king and the *oupahat*.

Among the hostages taken by the Siamese were four brothers of Deo Van Tri, son of a powerful White T'ai chieftain at Lai Chau. In revenge, Deo Van Tri's army,

composed largely of Chinese troops, descended on the un-
defended capital and burned it to the ground. Pavie, acting
with aplomb, saved Oun Kham's life by getting him away
in the nick of time aboard a canoe.

On their safe arrival at Pak Lay, Pavie had little difficulty
in persuading the king to forsake his worthless Siamese
protectorate in favor of one from France. Pavie also returned
unharmed the hostages to Deo Van Tri, who for the remainder
of his long life was a loyal friend of France. During the
interregnum that followed the sacking and later recapture of
Luang Prabang, France forced Siam to relinquish bit by bit
its "forward policy." The Sipsong Chau T'ai were turned over
to French control in 1888. Incidents in middle and southern
Laos continued between the Siamese and French for many
years, however, until finally the Siamese were compelled to
sign a treaty on October 3, 1893, renouncing all claims to
the left bank territories. (However, Siam did not formally
renounce all suzerainty over the kingdom of Luang Prabang
until the Franco-Siamese convention of 1904.) Although this
represented a real triumph for French proponents of empire
(who could point out that it had been achieved by a handful
of Frenchmen leading columns composed mainly of Vietnamese militia), the fact remained that the French were giving
legal status to a truncated Lao kingdom by formally aban-
doning Lan Xang's historic sovereignty over the right-bank
territories.

Oun Kham having died in 1895, his eldest son assumed
the throne under the name Zakarine (reign 1895–1904). An
administrative convention of December 3, 1895, became the
basis for France's presence in Luang Prabang. At his death,
Zakarine was succeeded by his eldest son, Sisavang Vong
(reign 1904–1959). Franco-Siamese conventions in 1902, 1904,
and 1907 attached limited territories on the right bank to
Luang Prabang and Champassak. The borders were delimited,
with Pavie himself taking part in missions in the Sipsong
Chau T'ai, with Burma (1896) and China (1896–1897). A joint
boundary commission with Siam delimited the western borders
of Sayaboury and Champassak between 1904 and 1907. The

French made Vieng Chan, renamed Vientiane, the seat of government again from 1900 onward (Map 3d).

FRANCE'S PROTECTORATE

French rule in Laos has been adequately described elsewhere. Whatever criticisms may be leveled at the French for their failure to equip Laos with a modern, industrialized economy, or to educate the masses of Lao and tribal peoples to the level of the metropolis, their rule in Laos was mild, with some exceptions. The French retained the traditional system of governance, appointing provincial governors and district officers, but allowing canton and village chiefs to be elected locally. The superstructure of parliamentary government invented by the French was a phenomenon of post–World War II Laos. In 1940, fewer than six hundred Frenchmen in Laos were governing slightly more than one million inhabitants.

Laos possessed few natural resources of value to the French and never accounted for more than 1 percent of total French exports from Indochina. The official French presence was usually manifested by the tax collector; although tax evasion was an absurdly simple matter in Laos, the sporadic attempts by the French administration to enforce a tax code that included both money payments and labor services (*corvée*) sparked some of the major rebellions against French rule. Notable for having been recorded, often by local French officials in sympathy with the rebels, were the rebellion among the Kha of the Bolovens Plateau led by the messianic Phou Mi Boun that lasted from 1895 to 1907; rebellion in Khammouane, 1898–1899; incidents in Champassak and Savannakhet, 1902; fresh rebellion by the Kha of southern Laos, led first by Ong Keo and then by Kommadan, 1910–1936; piracy in Sam Neua, 1914; rebellion among the Lu of Muong Sing led by Chao Fa Pha Ong Kham, 1914–1923; large-scale revolt among the Hmong in Xieng Khouang led by Tiao Pha Patchay, 1918–1922; and various incidents involving Vietnamese residents in the towns, 1930–1940.

Japanese Overlordship

But not until World War II was France's hold over its protectorate shaken in any substantial sense. With France's defeat by Germany in 1940, the Japanese moved to obtain important concessions from the Vichy government, whose governor general in Indochina, Admiral Jean Decoux, saw resistance as foolhardy and chose negotiations instead. The pact between Vichy and Tokyo of July 29, 1941, formalized the status quo. Although the Japanese were granted free movement of their troops everywhere in Indochina, Indochina was not occupied territory, and the French flag continued to fly. Decoux, who was described as secretive, choleric, and absolutely self-assured, saw his mission as preserving French sovereignty. Although not as personally devoted to Henri Philippe Pétain as some of his subordinates, he nevertheless encouraged the cult of the marshal as a means of accentuating France's responsibility for the native populations. He managed, by his handling of the Japanese, to limit French concessions, especially insofar as military collaboration was concerned, even when this meant defying orders from Vichy.

For Laos, the onset of Japan's overlordship in Southeast Asia was manifested primarily in the seizure from the French of the right-bank territories of Sayaboury and Champassak by Thailand (the new name for Siam). In the bloody little war that ensued, the French used Vietnamese troops. The arrogance of the Vietnamese caused a number of sons of leading Lao families to exile themselves in Thailand—whose government gave them protection—so as to organize a fight for Laos's independence.

To compensate King Sisavang Vong for the loss of his territory, the Vichy government agreed to formalize the protectorate. By the terms of a treaty signed by the king and Pétain on August 29, 1941, the kingdom of Luang Prabang included the provinces of Luang Prabang, Nam Tha, Phong Saly, Sam Neua, Xieng Khouang, and Vientiane. (Middle and southern Laos continued to be administered as before. The throne of Champassak had fallen vacant in 1900.) In addition, the French transformed the royal advisory council into a council of ministers, with Prince Phetsarath, a great-grandson of Oun Keo, as prime minister. Phetsarath was also named viceroy, a title that had lapsed at his father's death. The French retained control over defense, foreign affairs, and internal security.

As the war continued and Indochina remained totally isolated from France, Decoux may have become overconfident in his ability to outwit the Japanese. He seems to have acquired the notion that the Japanese would not dare to disrupt the status quo because, seeing that they were losing the war in the Pacific, they would want to rely on the good offices of France in bargaining with the Allies for surrender terms. In fact, Decoux may have believed that he could persuade the Japanese to evacuate Indochina of their own accord.

It may seem surprising that Charles de Gaulle, after he had set up his provisional government of the French Republic in liberated Paris in August 1944, did not simply cashier Decoux. In 1940, Decoux's nonresistance had saved lives, but by 1944 his obstinate Petainism and his public denunciations of Gaullism were threatening to make the whole French population of Indochina hostage to fate. Unlike Decoux, de Gaulle was convinced that the Japanese would move against the French administration in Indochina as soon as they had a pretext, and therefore felt an urgent need to organize an internal resistance movement for just such an eventuality. De Gaulle (as his subsequent actions in Africa proved) was no colonialist, but he needed the French Empire to face down the Allies and gain their acceptance of France as a postwar great power.[1]

In November, therefore, when the admiral got wind that de Gaulle was setting up an office in Paris to plan the liberation of Indochina, he cabled requesting confirmation of his powers. De Gaulle sent word that he was not only confirmed but ordered to maintain the status quo "for tactical reasons." On the night of December 22–23, Free French commandos under Captain L.-H. Ayrolles parachuted onto the Plain of Jars to establish the first of several resistance bases in Indochina.

Japanese military intelligence learned of these arrivals. Moreover, the Japanese high command became alarmed by heavy U.S. air raids on rail yards and Japanese shipping in Indochina on January 12, 1945, as possibly presaging an Allied landing. These events seem to have prompted the Supreme War Leadership Conference in Tokyo to decide on February 1 to move against the French; the Japanese did not trust the thirteen thousand French military in their midst in the event of an Allied landing.

On March 9, therefore, the Japanese declared the modus vivendi at an end and imprisoned all French people in Indochina. Although Decoux had drawn up plans for such a contingency, the Japanese move came so suddenly that the French were caught unprepared and only a handful managed to evade arrest.

Tokyo had left the time and manner of granting independence to the Indochinese, now that French administration had ended, to its commanders on the spot. The Japanese did not share a unified view on this question, and in Laos, at least, their offer of independence within the framework of the Greater East Asia Co-Prosperity Sphere was viewed as a mixed blessing. In Luang Prabang, Sisavang Vong and Crown Prince Savang Vatthana were served with a Japanese demand that they issue a proclamation of independence. Instead, Savang Vatthana decreed a mass uprising of his people against the Japanese. On this, the Japanese took steps to occupy the town and remove the crown prince to Saigon. They then compelled Sisavang Vong to issue a proclamation on April 8 declaring the 1941 treaty of protectorate null and void. Japanese officials replaced French *résidents* throughout Laos, symbolizing the fact that the Japanese had merely taken the place of the French.

Free Lao Versus Free France

The crucial result was that, in the absence of French administration, a struggle for power developed between the Lao exiles in Thailand and the Vietnamese residents in Laos. The guerrillas of the Free Lao, as they called themselves, moved into action almost immediatelly. The most significant of these groups was led by Oun Sananikone and crossed the Mekong at Savannakhet to begin distributing anti-French propaganda.

About fifty thousand Vietnamese residents were living in Laos in 1945, mainly in the large towns along the Mekong. They had been encouraged to establish themselves in Laos by the French, who recruited them as laborers, militia, and civil servants. Vietnamese held key positions in such departments of the administration as public works, posts and telegraph, customs, and police. After March 9, large numbers of them deserted from the Garde Indochinoise, taking their arms with them. The Japanese looked on these deserters sympathetically, even providing them with arms.

Phetsarath, who was much less favorably disposed to the French than were the king and crown prince, counted heavily on the Free Lao, who claimed to be in contact with U.S. agents of the Office of Strategic Services (OSS). In an attempt to reduce Vietnamese influence in Vientiane, Phetsarath took advantage of the Japanese commander's avowed intention of refraining from interfering in the internal affairs of Laos and replaced Vietnamese members of the civil service with Lao, sending Vietnamese and their families downriver to Thakhek. The opposition between Phetsarath and the Vietnamese led to a virtual paralysis of the ministries in Vientiane. Numerous incidents were reported; in Savannakhet, for instance, the Vietnamese denounced the *chao muong* to the Japanese for attempting to get his hands on the weapons of the Garde Indochinoise.

The French were not without their supporters among the Lao. Some of these went into the mountains to join the Free French commandos, at great risk to themselves since the Japanese had decreed the death penalty for anyone found assisting the French cause. Among these were Prince Boun Oum, heir to the defunct throne of Champassak, who felt that immediate independence would turn Laos into a battleground between Thailand and Vietnam, and Phoui Sananikone, *chao khoueng* of Nam Tha, who escaped into China.

With Japanese surrender imminent, the struggle for power in Laos, as elsewhere in Indochina, approached a climax, hastened by one of the strangest decisions in great-power summitry. At the Potsdam Conference of July-August, the United States, Britain, and the Soviet Union, in the absence of de Gaulle, decided that British and Chinese Nationalist forces would enter Indochina to accept the surrender of Japanese forces there. This decision ensured what Decoux had feared most—a power vacuum. Three days after the emperor ordered Japanese forces to surrender, General Yuitsu Tsuchihashi, commander of the Thirty-eighth army and acting governor general of Indochina, in a telegram cited by Paul Isoart,[2] ordered Japanese forces to hand over power to the independent Indochinese governments. At this point, British and Chinese forces had still not entered Indochina and the Free French were still in tiny numbers.

De Gaulle, meanwhile, was having to obtain recognition from his allies of French sovereignty over Indochina. President Franklin D. Roosevelt had never looked favorably on restoration of French sovereignty over Indochina, but at the end of August when he visited Washington, de Gaulle received a personal promise from President Harry S Truman that the United States did not oppose the return of the French army and French authority to Indochina now that Japan had been defeated. De Gaulle's relationship with Winston Churchill had been prickly, but the British commanders responsible for Indochina at war's end did all they could to assist the French.

The critical place in terms of political authority was obviously Luang Prabang. An artillery officer of Swiss origin, Hans Imfeld, acting for the Free French, landed at Luang Prabang on August 29 and discovered that the town had already been evacuated by the Japanese. In a meeting with the crown prince, Imfeld received assurances that the monarch maintained his attachment to France, coupled with a plea that he, Imfeld, do everything possible to forestall the entry into Laos of a Chinese occupation army. The local population, remembering perhaps the Ho, were already building canoes to escape. The following day Imfeld received a declaration

The royal palace, Luang Prabang. (Photo in author's collection)

from the king himself affirming that the protectorate had never ceased to exist.

Meanwhile at Vientiane, where the Vietnamese had started to distribute anti-French tracts, events were threatening to get beyond Phetsarath's control. The prime minister had released the former French resident from prison, informing him that as the Vichy government no longer existed he represented no authority whatsoever. To prevent excesses, however, Phetsarath was obliged to decree strong measures for preserving law and order. He hoped, from his contacts with Free Lao agents in the town, that an interallied commission would soon arrive in Vientiane to settle Laos's future status.

When he learned that the king had handed a French agent a declaration stating that the protectorate was still in force, Phetsarath was furious. One of Phetsarath's main objectives was to attach the southern provinces to the kingdom of Luang Prabang, thereby unifying Laos. He obtained the agreement of the governors of these provinces to this step. The king, however, whose title was still King of Lan Xang of Luang Prabang (Somdet Phra Chao Lan-Xang Hom-Khao Nakhone Luang-Prabang), did not reply to Phetsarath's request for authority to issue a unification proclamation. Phetsarath thereupon acted unilaterally to name Oun commissioner of the southern provinces.

Enter the Viet Minh

Meanwhile, in Vietnam the Viet Minh—the national resistance organization formed by the Indochinese Communist Party (ICP), founded in 1930 under Ho Chi Minh—had moved quickly to fill the vacuum. Ho proclaimed himself president of an independent Vietnam on September 2. He naturally was alarmed by French preparations to reassert their sovereignty over Indochina and suspected them of plotting to move their forces up the Mekong to outflank his base in northern Vietnam, as he told a U.S. OSS officer at the time.[3] He sent Viet Minh agents into the Mekong River towns of Laos to forestall an imminent French reoccupation and ordered the execution of any Vietnamese in the pay of the French who assisted them. In towns like Thakhek and Paksane, pro–Viet Minh sentiment was running so high that the red and yellow-starred flag of Ho's republic was already flying there.

One of the Viet Minh agents sent into Laos by Ho contacted Phetsarath who, in his temporary isolation, would be amenable to an offer to help. The primary intermediary of this help was Phetsarath's younger half brother, prince Souphanouvong, who had been working in Vietnam as a civil engineer and was at that moment preparing to march across the Annamite Mountains with a Viet Minh bodyguard of fifty armed men.

Souphanouvong's first objective was Savannakhet, where Oun's guerrillas had been in charge since the Japanese surrender. The Free Lao, disappointed at the failure of the OSS to deliver promised arms, had created a Committee for Free Lao under Oun. After Souphanouvong's arrival on October

8, this committee was renamed the Committee for Independent Laos (Khana Lao Issara) and reshuffled, with Phetsarath as honorary president, Souphanouvong as president, and Oun as vice-president. This marked the first step toward establishing an independent government. Souphanouvong signed an order on the same day creating a liberation army.

Meanwhile, in Vientiane the situation had evolved with equal rapidity. Phetsarath's supporters had established a Defense Committee. When, however, a message arrived from Luang Prabang on October 10 that Phetsarath had been stripped of his titles of viceroy and prime minister, he sent a message saying he would follow the king's orders. He then took this telegram and one he had received on September 7 informing him that the king had placed his kingdom under the French and gave them to the people and civil servants. He announced that he could take no further part in his country's affairs. On October 12, the Defense Committee voted a provisional constitution, a provisional people's assembly, and the nomination of a government to be known as the Lao Issara (Free Laos) under Panya Khammao Vilay, governor of Vientiane. Eight days later, when Sisavang Vong refused to endorse the Lao Issara, the provisonal people's assembly voted to depose him.

An agreement concluded on October 30 between Khammao and Tran Duc Vinh, the official representative of Ho's government, and countersigned by Souphanouvong as commander in chief of the Lao liberation army, allowed Viet Minh units to operate in Laos, "given the community of the major interests of Vietnam and Laos and the necessity of safeguarding their common independence."[4] The practical effect of this agreement was to give a decisive voice at every level to the Viet Minh cadres, known as technical advisers, who had accompanied Souphanouvong from Vietnam. Souphanouvong also was made foreign minister in Khammao's government.

While Thakhek was in the hands of armed Vietnamese and Vientiane was under strong Vietnamese influence, the situation at Luang Prabang was different. The royal capital had virtually no Vietnamese residents, and there the Lao

Issara were able to conduct affairs on their own, with the help of Chinese forces that had begun arriving in late September. On the night of November 4, a small band of Free Lao partisans under Chao Sisoumang Sisaleumsak forced their way into the barracks of the Garde Indochinoise and gained access to a large stock of arms and ammunition. Imfeld, whose command post was kept surrounded by Chinese troops, was powerless to intervene. Then the Free Lao partisans marched on the royal palace, knocking down a statue of Pavie on the way. There was some shooting in the air, and Sisavang Vong was told that since he had refused a request from the government to abdicate voluntarily, he had been deposed by order of that government.

The situation in Xieng Khouang was even more confused than those in Vientiane and Luang Prabang. On April 12, four days after the Japanese-sponsored declaration of independence, Vietnamese at Khang Khay, armed with stolen Japanese weapons, announced a decision to proclaim a prefecture (*phu*) with allegiance to Vietnam. However, a pro-French secretary Chao Say Kham, aided by a youth corps he had organized, was able to prevent the Vietnamese from taking over Xieng Khouang town where the seals of administration were kept, until the arrival of the first French commandos. The balance of forces in Xieng Khouang was made more precarious by the fact that the Hmong, although in majority sympathetic to the French, harbored a minority faction that supported the Viet Minh.

A small force under Sing Ratanasamay, a Free Lao leader who had been made defense minister in the Lao Issara government, approached up Route 7 from the west and reached the Plain of Jars on November 26. This force succeeded in taking Xieng Khouang town two days later, while French commandos and Hmong guerrillas skirmished with Viet Minh patrols farther east. But Ho, preoccupied with staging a show of strength in Hanoi, was unable to make good on his pledge of support for the Lao Issara, and, in the absence of fresh Viet Minh troops, Sing and his tiny force were compelled to relinquish Xieng Khouang to the French, by then heavily reinforced, on January 26, 1946.

A month later, on February 28, a Franco-Chinese agreement provided for the complete withdrawal of Chinese forces from Laos by March 31 and enabled the French forces, who had mustered in Pakse (in the British-occupied zone south of the 16th parallel), to begin moving north. They reoccupied Savannakhet, which Oun's partisans decided to abandon without a fight for fear of a massacre of Lao on both sides, on March 17. But four days later Souphanouvong and his Vietnamese followers stood their ground at Thakhek. The battle was unequal: troops with rudimentary weapons against tanks and aircraft. The fighting left the town in ruins and a reported three thousand dead. Souphanouvong was seriously wounded by a British Spitfire that strafed his boat as he fled across the river. Thinking he was sure to die, he urged Oun to continue the struggle.

The Associated State of Laos

Phetsarath, who had withdrawn to Luang Prabang, refused a Lao Issara offer to take the regency and, in a last noble gesture, invited Sisavang Vong to assume office as constitutional monarch and give legitimacy to all that had been done, as Hugh Toye put it. The king finally agreed and was reinstated with due ceremony on April 23, the day before the French reoccupied Vientiane with only minor skirmishing. The Lao Issara ministers, after setting fire to a few government buildings, fled across the Mekong to Thailand, following the example set by virtually the entire Vietnamese population. They had forestalled a plan by the Vietnamese to burn Vientiane to the ground in retaliation for the French burning of the Vietnamese district of Thakhek. By September, the French tricolor flew once more over the two capitals and all the provincial capitals of Laos.

On August 27, the French and Crown Prince Savang Vatthana signed a modus vivendi that recognized the unity of Laos, thereby giving reality to Phetsarath's dream. Prince Boun Oum agreed to merge his royal rights into the sovereignty of the Kingdom of Laos. The crown prince took charge of a provisional national government, and in January 1947 elections were held for a constituent assembly. A constitution drawn up by this assembly was promulgated on May 11, and Laos became a constitutional monarchy within the French Union. The French, meanwhile, gained the retrocession to Laos by Thailand of the right-bank territories.

A Franco-Lao general convention signed in Paris by Sisavang Vong in July 1949 accorded the kingdom greater latitude in foreign affairs. For the first time, the royal flag of Laos, a white three-headed elephant on a red field, flew in the French capital. U.S. recognition of the Associated State of Laos followed on February 4, 1950.

SCHISM IN THE INDEPENDENCE MOVEMENT

Resistance to the reimposition of French rule, kindled in the dramatic events of 1945-1946, soon flamed up anew. Events in Indochina had overtaken de Gaulle's liberal proposals from as early as 1945 for new relations between France and the countries of Indochina. A French government statement of March 24, 1945, had replaced French Empire with French Union, and the latter was given substance in the constitutional referendum of October 27, 1946. But by then de Gaulle had been out of office for nine months, and his place had been taken by people of narrower vision.

Nevertheless, in Laos at least, French efforts at conciliation with the nationalists bore fruit. Discreet overtures toward the Lao Issara in Bangkok, where the exiled government, now joined by Phetsarath, had its seat, suggested the possibility of an amnesty. Gradually, a division of opinion appeared within the Lao Issara ranks over the practical issue of whether to cooperate with the French. Souphanouvong had made clear his refusal to accept the new political set-up in Vientiane, and as early as February 1949 he had established a separate political front for the guerrilla army he commanded, the Progressive People's Organization. But Souphanouvong's readiness to embrace an alliance with the Viet Minh repelled most of his colleagues, including his half brother, Prince Souvanna Phouma, who held the portfolio of public works, and no doubt hastened their decision to split with him and return home. On October 24, 1949, the Lao Issara accordingly announced its formal dissolution and Souvanna Phouma and twenty-five of the more moderate figures in the movement returned home to Vientiane. Phetsarath remained behind, bitter over being deposed as viceroy and over not having his title restored in the 1947 constitution.

Souphanouvong now took the Vietnamese road to power from which he never deviated to the day he was named president of the new people's republic in December 1975. In 1949 he moved his headquarters from Bangkok to northern Vietnam, and on August 13, 1950, he presided over the First Resistance Congress, convened in secrecy somewhere near the borders of Phong Saly, Sam Neua, and Luang Prabang provinces. The congress organized a resistance government of Pathet Lao, with Souphanouvong as prime minister and including a number of other clandestine figures, such as a Lao-Vietnamese *métisse* named Kaysone Phomvihane, who had been a member of the ICP and who had been active in the Laos-Vietnam border area while Souphanouvong was in Bangkok.

When the Vietnamese reconstituted their Communist party in February 1951, naming it the Vietnamese Workers party, Souphanouvong and the Lao Communists were in attendance. The following month, a joint conference of national united fronts in Vietnam, Laos, and Cambodia announced formation of an alliance "aimed at wiping out the French colonialists, defeating the American interventionists, and punishing the traitorous puppets, and gaining genuine independence for the three peoples and contributing to the maintenance of world peace."[5]

LAOS IN THE FIRST INDOCHINA WAR

While the French government was taking the first steps toward giving Laos a constitutional government, France and the Viet Minh were engaged in the bloody, eight-year struggle known as the First Indochina War. Hostilities began with the spectacular naval bombardment of Haiphong by the French and the evacuation of Hanoi by Ho's government, rupturing a fragile modus vivendi worked out in March 1946.

Despite official optimism, the war grew more and more difficult for the French as Ho and his defense minister, Vo Nguyen Giap, built up their forces in the mountains. The Chinese Communists reached the Vietnam border, which meant a sanctuary and secure supply lines for the Viet Minh, and a string of disastrous French defeats soon followed. The arrival of Marshal de Lattre de Tassigny in Vietnam enabled the French to infuse new spirit and strategy into their war effort. For a time the French, bolstered by increasing U.S. aid, seemed to have turned the tide against Ho and Giap. But after the marshal's death in January 1952 the Viet Minh again seized the initiative, and in winter 1952-1953 they launched their most ambitious offensive to date.

Then, in April 1953 the Viet Minh invaded Laos, which was defended by only twelve thousand Lao Territorials and three thousand French troops. The first prong of the Viet Minh invading force comprised fifteen battalions drawn from the 308th, 312th, and 316th divisions and drove through Sam Neua and across the Plain of Jars. The second prong comprised five crack battalions and drove down the valley of the Nam Hou. On April 28, these forces joined about thirty miles from Luang Prabang. The French rushed in reinforcements by aircraft, stretching their logistical capability to the limit.

In the face of concern for the king's safety, a blind monk in Luang Prabang prophesied that the Viet Minh would not enter the town. The U.S. chargé d'affaires in Saigon, however, was certain that Luang Prabang would fall and urged the crown prince and his father to leave the capital. He added that he looked forward to calling upon them "at such a place of residence as you may choose." Savang and Sisavang Vong held firm, much to the relief of the local population. The Viet Minh invaders faded away again as swiftly as they had come.

The Viet Minh invasion of Laos in 1953 made a mockery of the French strategy of holding strong points deep in the mountains of Tonkin in the belief that these interfered with Viet Minh troop movements. Ho and Giap proved that they

could move sizeable forces anywhere in Indochina with im-
punity and demonstrated that they had greater mobility than
the French with their aircraft and vehicles. In Washington,
President Dwight D. Eisenhower expressed his disappointment
to his principal advisers; until this invasion, he told them,
he had imagined that the French would be able eventually
to overcome their enemies, but the invasion demonstrated
that neither the French nor the U.S. troops could possibly
hold Indochina on their own. As one of his successors was
to find following the Communists' Tet offensive fifteen years
later, Eisenhower concluded that the war was unwinnable on
the terms on which it was being fought and he foresaw the
loss of the remainder of Southeast Asia if it continued this
way. The invasion also allowed the Viet Minh to gain un-
disputed control over Sam Neua, whose governor their forces
had executed in a "people's trial." They immediately set about
giving slightly more substance to Souphanouvong's claim to
lead a resistance government by making this its territorial
capital. This thin slice of Laos was an opening wedge.

INDEPENDENCE

The sovereignty of Laos remained centered on Luang
Prabang and Vientiane. In response to further demands made
on them by Souvanna Phouma, who had become prime
minister in November 1951, coupled with U.S. pressure on
a succession of weak Fourth Republic governments in Paris,
the French removed all remaining qualification on Laos's
independence by the Franco-Laotian treaty of October 22,
1953.

After the rainy season of 1953, the Viet Minh 325th
Division invaded central Laos, using trails it was to get to
know well. It briefly occupied Thakhek, withdrawing when
the French rushed in reinforcements. By the end of 1953,
however, the focus of the war was shifting to a strong point
the French were building up in the valley of Dien Bien Phu.
In January and February 1954, the Viet Minh 308th Division
made a lightning thrust from its base in Tonkin toward Luang

Prabang, forcing the French to divert air support from their Dien Bien Phu operation.

French public opinion was beginning to swing against the war. Especially after the conclusion of an armistice in Korea on July 27, 1953, which left France alone among the big powers fighting the Communists in Asia, many French people came to feel that a similar process of negotiation—long drawn out and frustrating as it was—might produce a formula whereby France could disengage from Indochina. Such sentiment was strengthened by hints, and eventually by explicit offers, from Communist governments. The Soviet Union had embarked on peaceful coexistence with the West. China, having ended its involvement in Korea, professed its peaceful intentions toward Asian states. In summer 1953 radio broadcasts from Peking and Moscow hinted at the possibility of a truce in Indochina. Most significant, in an interview published in a Swedish newspaper in November Ho himself hinted at the possibility of an armistice based on French recognition of the independence of Vietnam.

At the Big Four conference in Berlin in January 1954, the United States, Britain, France, and the Soviet Union agreed to convene a conference in Geneva of countries that had been involved in the Korean War to try to find a lasting political solution to the Korean problem and to discuss peace in Indochina. When the Korean phase of the Geneva Conference convened on April 26, no agreement had been reached on what countries would be represented in the discussion of the Indochina question. Soviet Foreign Minister Vyacheslav Molotov suggested that the conference include both the Democratic Republic of Vietnam (DRV) (recognized by the Communists) and the State of Vietnam (recognized by France, the United States, and some thirty-five other countries), and the two other Associated States of Indochina, namely, Laos and Cambodia. On May 3, official invitations were dispatched to the three Associated States and the DRV by the conference cochairmen, Britain and the USSR. The DRV delegation, led by Prime Minister Pham Van Dong, arrived in Geneva from East Berlin on May 4 and immediately demanded that invitations be issued to the Pathet Lao and Khmer Issarak resistance governments in Laos and Cambodia.

LAOS AT THE 1954 GENEVA CONFERENCE

The demand for representation of the resistance governments received support on May 6 from the Chinese, whose delegation had been participating in the Korean phase under Foreign Minister Chou En-lai. At the first plenary session on Indochina on May 8, the day following the fall of Dien Bien Phu to the Viet Minh, Dong devoted the major part of his speech to the demand for the seating of the Pathet Lao and their Cambodian counterparts, the Khmer Issarak. The DRV delegation had come secretly prepared, since it included a young Laotian traveling on a Vietnamese passport, Nouhak Phoumsavanh, foreign minister in the Pathet Lao government. Dong's demand was sharply contested by the delegation of the royal government led by Phoui Sananikone.

The representational issue, involving at its core the question of the vestiture of sovereignty of Laos and Cambodia, marked a fundamental difference in the situation of Laos from that of Vietnam. In the former, a solidly established independent government faced a rebel movement whose control of territory, as well as its claims of popular backing, depended on the intervention of a foreign power. In the latter, two rival governments, each recognized by opposing foreign powers, vied for sovereignty. In this respect, Laos was much more fortunate than Vietnam.

The DRV delegation stuck with its demands, which were given pro forma support by Molotov and Chou, until May 25, when Dong in a major switch of strategy proposed a complete and simultaneous cease-fire throughout Indochina, to be followed by the regrouping of regular military forces into zones established by the conference. Such zones, he said, should be economically and politically viable and controlled by a single administration. The DRV, in fact, was proposing the partitioning of Vietnam and Laos.

Dong had clearly been persuaded by the Soviets and Chinese of the untenability of demanding recognition by the conference of the resistance governments in Laos and Cambodia. On June 16, Chou indicated to British Foreign Secretary Anthony Eden that China was prepared to recognize Laos and Cambodia as independent states "in the same manner as India and Burma," provided that the United States was not permitted to establish military bases on their territory. China's interest lay in preventing Ho's government from dominating all of Indochina.[6] In an oversight heavy with consequences for subsequent U.S. involvement in Indochina, U.S. Secretary of State John Foster Dulles—who quixotically refused to shake Chou's hand—did not perceive the divergence of interests between China and the DRV.

In contrast to Chou, who showed he was quite at home amid the complexities of Indochinese politics and operated backstage throughout the conference, actively sounding out positions here and floating trial balloons there, the U.S. delegation assumed a passive role, accepting with bad grace the compromises worked out by others. As far as Laos was concerned, the major contribution of the U.S. delegation (a positive one) was to keep attention focused on the Viet Minh presence in the country; the delegation at one point read into the record a roster of battalion and regimental designations of Viet Minh units still in Laos at the time the conference met. This presentation helped force the DRV to admit publicly the presence of its people's volunteer forces in Laos. The Viet Minh divisions in Laos were recruited from among the minority tribespeople who inhabited the mountain areas that had been under Viet Minh control since the beginning of the war.

Phoui's delegation faced the difficult task of upholding the sovereignty of Laos throughout the negotiations, which in their military aspects involved solely the representatives of the two opposing military commands, the French Union forces and the Viet Minh. In a meeting at Chou's villa between Phoui and Dong on June 23, however, Dong agreed to the withdrawal of Viet Minh forces from Laos and the retention by the Laotians of a modest French military training mission. He was concerned that no military alliance be formed between Laos and the United States, and asked Phoui to request

Souvanna Phouma to meet soon with Souphanouvong for a discussion of political issues.

In the military talks, however, the Viet Minh showed their true face, advancing maximum demands on the French where Laos was concerned. They pressed for a regrouping zone for Pathet Lao forces comprising almost one-half the country, adjoining the entire length of the Laos-Vietnam border. At this time, the line of partition in Vietnam was still under negotiation, but the Viet Minh were seeking to obtain a Pathet Lao–controlled zone adjacent to their traditional base areas in northern Vietnam that also abutted southern Vietnam. When the French showed the Viet Minh proposal to Molotov's military advisers the latter called it absurd.

Chou, active as ever, presented the Laotians with modifications to the Viet Minh proposals during the final, climactic days of the negotiations. The Viet Minh, in addition to claiming about half the country for their clients, were also putting forth feelers for a coalition government in Laos. Phoui informed the French that his delegation would not under any circumstances agree to such sweeping concessions. And in the end, Laos emerged the best among the four Indochinese governments represented at Geneva, after Cambodia, where the claims of the tiny Viet Minh puppet group were too ludicrous to hold water and which consequently emerged intact.

The military agreements were signed by the French and the Viet Minh on July 20, 1954. The conference also issued a final declaration of the participants. The agreement on Laos provided for the regrouping of the Pathet Lao in the provinces of Phong Saly and Sam Neua. The royal government, furthermore, unilaterally committed itself to provide special representation in the provincial administration there for the Pathet Lao during the period between the cease-fire and the next general elections. In contrast to the settlement in Vietnam, where a partition line had been drawn at the 17th parallel dividing the country into approximately equal parts with two separate and equal temporary administrations, the agreement on Laos did not use the term *partition* and clearly left the authority of the royal government in force. The vast majority of the people of Laos could well be satisfied with the outcome: The furthest thing from their leaders' minds was to allow foreign military bases on their soil or to join a military alliance.

NOTES

1. Don Cook, *Charles de Gaulle: A Biography* (New York: G. P. Putnam's Sons, 1983), p. 285.

2. Paul Isoart, "Aux Origines d'une Guerre," in Paul Isoart, ed., *L'Indochine Française, 1940–1945* (Paris: Presses Universitaires de France, 1982), p. 59.

3. Archimedes L. A. Patti, *Why Viet Nam: Prelude to America's Albatross* (Berkeley: University of California Press, 1980), p. 348. Ho mentioned Vientiane and Savannakhet as areas of particular concern. French agents were certainly active in Vientiane; Savannakhet, however, was under Free Lao control at the time. In Laos, as in Vietnam, Ho regarded rival nationalist movements as threats to his drive for power.

4. France, Archives SOM, Fonds de la Résidence Supérieure au Laos, Carton F19, Bulletin de Renseignements no. 18, Savannakhet, April 14, 1946.

5. Allan W. Cameron, ed., *Viet-Nam Crisis: A Documentary History* (Ithaca, N.Y.: Cornell University Press, 1971), p. 183.

6. An interest that later extended to cultivating close bilateral relations with the National Liberation Front of South Vietnam.

4

Independence to the Second Geneva Conference (1954–1962)

By 1954 the Kingdom of Laos had regained its independence and was able to participate in the Geneva Conference as a fully sovereign nation. The successors of the Indochinese Communist party, however, were not reconciled to an independent Laos outside their orbit. Using the northern half of Vietnam, now under their legal control, as a formidable base area and arguing that the United States had replaced France as the colonial presence in Indochina, they set out to change Laos's status. Quite apart from their plan to reunify Vietnam under Communist control, they embarked on a revolution in Laos, using the Pathet Lao fighting units as pawns.

IMPLEMENTATION OF
THE 1954 GENEVA AGREEMENT

The weak points in the final agreement on Laos reached at Geneva were revealed almost immediately. The modalities of demobilizing the Pathet Lao troops or of integrating them into the royal army were left to further negotiations and the machinery set up to verify the withdrawal of foreign troops was inadequate. Conflict initially arose over two issues. First, a contradiction was inherent between the royal government's view and that of the Pathet Lao. The royal government contended that as a sovereign entity it was entitled to exercise its normal functions anywhere in Laos—including stationing its troops, after the withdrawal of the French, in Phong Saly and Sam Neua. The Pathet Lao, on the other hand, held the view that until their special representation in the adminis-tration of the two provinces had been agreed upon, they were empowered to exercise exclusive authority in the re-grouping zone. Second, a further contradiction existed between the royal government's stand that the general elections sched-uled for 1955 should be held in conformity with existing laws and the Pathet Lao view that, as they had not taken part in the voting for the National Assembly, they were not bound by laws passed by that body and were entitled to a say in drafting a new electoral law.

The Geneva Conference had established an International Commission for Supervision and Control (ICSC), composed of delegations from India, Canada, and Poland. The ICSC was hamstrung in its attempts to enforce the cease-fire agree-ments by its remoteness from the scene, by its dependence on facilities provided by the two parties, by thinly concealed Pathet Lao obstruction of its work, and finally by the influence of the ideological split within its own ranks on the tenor of its reports to the Geneva cochairmen. The ICSC was unable to verify the withdrawal of Viet Minh troops from Laos and had to rely on a statement by the chief of the Viet Minh–Pathet Lao delegation to the Joint Commission that the high command of the Vietnam People's Army had decided to withdraw all "volunteers" from Laos within the 120-day period prescribed by the cease-fire agreement.

LAOS AND SEATO

The last year of France's agony in Indochina had led to a debate in Washington about whether the United States should intervene more directly than by providing military aid to the French and the Associated States, which it had been doing under the so-called pentalateral agreements since 1950. President Eisenhower finally decided that U.S. interests did not lie with committing armed forces to the conflict; he saw it primarily as a colonial war and therefore one unwinnable by an outside power, and he recognized that U.S. intervention would be highly unpopular with Congress so soon after the armistice in Korea. Furthermore, he saw that U.S. intervention risked isolating the United States from its traditional allies, especially Great Britain.

Foreseeing that the non-Communist states of Southeast Asia would be left dangerously exposed to Communist aggression if the French withdrew from Indochina (a constant worry) or were forced to accept a partitioned Indochina in armistice negotiations (an outcome that the French defeat at Dien Bien Phu seemed to make inevitable), Secretary of State Dulles was already thinking about establishing a standing alliance for the defense of Southeast Asia before the war ended. In Dulles's view, China was the threat to Southeast Asia. Mao Tse-tung's victory barely five years before had led to recriminations in the United States about "losing China" and had made Eisenhower's administration sensitive to the possibility of losing further Asian territory to the Communists. The Chinese Communists had provided to the Viet Minh some of the massive quantities of U.S. arms they had captured from the nationalists during the civil war, and this action lent some credence to the theory that China was a threat to independent Southeast Asia. Actually, as we have seen, China came to Geneva wanting good relations with Laos and the other countries of Indochina.

When the Southeast Asia Treaty Organization (SEATO) was formed at Manila in September 1954, its members included the Philippines and Pakistan, as well as Thailand, the United States, Britain, France, Australia, and New Zealand. As the Laotian government had accepted an obligation at Geneva not to join any military alliance, the SEATO signatories adopted a protocol to their treaty unanimously designating Laos for purposes of Article IV—the operational article committing members "to act to meet the common danger" in the event of aggression against any one of them. By this roundabout way Laos was included under the SEATO umbrella for purposes of containment.

Royal Lao Army soldiers at ease, Vientiane. (Photo in author's collection)

Pursuing this policy with religious zeal,[1] the State Department lobbied successfully for a build-up of military aid
to Vientiane. However, the U.S. military establishment saw
little value in increasing Laos's army from its wartime strength
of 17,500 persons. As late as 1958, Defense Department
documents showed the Laotian army as "not within force

objectives." At State Department insistence, however, its armed strength was increased to twenty-five thousand persons and a training mission in civilian disguise, known as the Program Evaluation Office (PEO), was set up in Vientiane.

Non-Communist Laotians harbored few illusions about the danger they faced, but they saw this danger differently. Crown Prince Savang Vatthana told U.S. Ambassador Donald Heath that he did not place much faith in the SEATO treaty: Guarantees against external aggression were insufficient against Communist tactics, he said, and Laos had more need of guarantees of constitutional government. With a secure base behind them in North Vietnam,[2] and with North Vietnamese political and military support guaranteed by the tripartite alliance of 1951, the small Pathet Lao movement was out to achieve maximum gains in Laos.

During the Geneva negotiations, the Viet Minh and Chinese delegations had hinted, in talks with the Laotians, at the possibility of forming a coalition government to include the Pathet Lao. Phoui's delegation had succeeded in preventing the French from committing the Laotians to such an eventuality. Rumors of a possible coalition had reached Dulles's ears, however, and he was sufficiently alarmed to cable instructions to the U.S. delegation on June 23 that the "Laotians should be warned particularly against striking any bargain with Prince Souphanouvong which might lead them to a coalition."[3]

The U.S. State Department—seeing Laos as a place to contain an aggressive China—pursued a policy of confrontation against the Pathet Lao. Some Laotians, however, doubted the wisdom of such a policy. The problem with confrontation, they felt, was that it inevitably pushed the Pathet Lao into the embrace of the North Vietnamese, whereas the only chance of success for the nationalists lay in splitting the Pathet Lao off from the North Vietnamese. Prince Souvanna Phouma, half brother of Prince Souphanouvong and the prime minister at the time of the Geneva Conference, claimed that he could bring about this division and became the central figure in international efforts to neutralize Laos for the next two decades. He believed that he could persuade Souphanouvong to negotiate a political settlement that would eliminate the Pathet Lao's dependence on North Vietnam by giving them a share of power in his government. One of Souvanna Phouma's first acts after the ceasefire had been signed was to fly to Khang Khay, the town on the Plain of Jars that was to become the venue of many such meetings on "neutral" ground.

For the next three years, negotiations between the Vientiane government and the Pathet Lao went on more or less continuously. The immediate focus was the question of the administration of the provinces of Sam Neua and Phong Saly; behind this issue lay the larger one of Pathet Lao participation in the political life of the kingdom. As the negotiations proceeded, cabinets succeeded one another in Vientiane and armed clashes took place in the two contested provinces. Moreover, the Pathet Lao boycotted the elections for the National Assembly in December 1955.

Souvanna Phouma and his supporters in Vientiane pushed ahead doggedly with the often thankless task of simultaneously (1) attempting to negotiate a settlement with the Pathet Lao, who claimed to be the country's genuine patriots; (2) keeping in line the Vientiane politicians who advocated a tough stance against the Communists; and (3) maintaining a sufficiently pro-Western posture to satisfy U.S. Ambassador J. Graham Parsons, who, faithful to his instructions from Washington, did all he could do to thwart the establishment of a coalition. Invariably, Souvanna Phouma came away from his periodic meetings with the Pathet Lao negotiators exuding optimism that a settlement was within reach, only to give way to pessimism when the Pathet Lao behavior failed to conform to his image of a pliable movement susceptible to his moderating influence.

To counter the growing power of the Right (increasingly identified with Thailand), Souvanna Phouma used the 1955 Bandung Asian-African Conference and visits to Peking and Hanoi in 1956 to extract from the North Vietnamese leaders (then in one of their pro-Chinese phases) verbal assurances that the Pathet Lao question was essentially an internal affair and that relations between neighboring states should be

governed by the principle of noninterference. The cause of
reconciliation among the Laotians received a boost from the
return to Laos in 1956 of Prince Phetsarath, who urged his
brothers to bury their differences. Even so, the negotiations
were arduous and threatened to break down on more than
one occasion.

THE FIRST COALITION

Finally, in November 1957, two sets of agreements were
concluded between the Pathet Lao and the Vientiane government. Under the military agreements completed on November 2, fifteen hundred members of the Pathet Lao fighting
forces were to be integrated into the royal army and the
remainder honorably discharged. The political accords signed
on November 12 provided for the establishment of a government of national union and the reintegration of the two
contested provinces on a compromise basis: One would have
a governor from Vientiane seconded by a Pathet Lao deputy
governor and the other, the reverse. Article 8 of this agreement
provided that Souphanouvong would make a declaration of
transfer of the two provinces and their military and civilian
personnel to the royal authority, and Article 9 provided that
the prime minister would give his accord to the exercise of
free democratic rights throughout the country by the Neo
Lao Hak Sat (NLHS), or Lao Patriotic Front, the political
party formed by the Pathet Lao on January 6, 1956.

On November 18, in a ceremony in the garden of the
royal residence in Vientiane, Souphanouvong formally restored
to Crown Prince Savang Vatthana the two provinces. On the
following day the National Assembly in a special session gave
its unanimous vote of approval to the new government, which
included Souphanouvong as minister of reconstruction and
planning and Phoumi Vongvichit as minister of religion and
fine arts.

The first coalition lasted barely eight months. Its main
achievement was to hold national elections in May 1958. The
elections were for twenty-one new seats in the National
Assembly (raising the total to fifty-nine), representing not

only Sam Neua and Phong Saly, but also other areas that were judged to have been underrepresented. The results gave the NLHS and its ally, the Santiphab (Peace) party, a resounding triumph; Souphanouvong himself received more votes than any other candidate.

A large issue in the electoral campaign had been widespread allegations of corruption against the U.S. aid program. The program was so massive in relation to Laos's tiny economy that it was virtually uncontrollable, and its frequent abuses resulted in the enrichment of a few. This issue certainly played into the hands of the NLHS, which claimed to represent genuine democracy. But some right-wing politicians, mostly those younger and better educated than the old-line politicians, saw in the issue of corruption a means of attaining power. These people included a number of military officers.

From summer 1958 to that of 1959, a number of developments followed that were unfavorable to Hanoi and Peking. First, the majority of ICSC commissioners voted to adjourn sine die. The ICSC, although ineffective in enforcing the military clauses of the Geneva agreements, at least provided a forum of first appeal in cases of armed clashes, and thus exerted a moderating influence on both sides. Second, and more ominous, the political situation in Vientiane evolved in an unforeseen manner. Souvanna Phouma's coalition government, when threatened with a cutoff of U.S. aid resulting from the outcry over misuse, fell on July 23, triggering a full-scale parliamentary crisis. The new government headed by Phoui Sananikone accelerated the swing to the Right, while still professing neutrality.

Previous overtures for establishing diplomatic relations with Peking and Moscow had been politely deflected by the Laotian leaders, mindful of the alarm such a move would provoke in Washington. But the new government, casting aside any considerations of balance in foreign relations, announced the establishment of diplomatic relations with the Chinese Nationalist government on Taiwan and the South Vietnamese government of President Ngo Dinh Diem. Souvanna Phouma was sent as ambassador to France, and Souphanouvong remained in Vientiane as chairman of the National Assembly. There, he had to contend with the rising influence of a group calling themselves the Committee for the Defense of the National Interests (CDNI), who were able to turn the NLHS's success in exploiting the corruption issue (as demonstrated in the elections results) to their own advantage by calling for a strongly anti-Communist policy.

THE START OF THE SECOND INDOCHINA WAR

Ho's government in Hanoi, all this while, was nearing a fateful decision regarding its future course of action in South Vietnam. Diem's government in Saigon had survived against all odds and had refused to open discussions with Hanoi on holding the Vietnam-wide elections in July 1956 as provided for in the final declaration of the Geneva Conference. Furthermore, as a result of the withdrawal of Viet Minh regular units north of the demarcation line, the clandestine Communist political network in the South was in danger of dismemberment at the hands of Diem's police. The secret agents Hanoi sent on mission to the South came back reporting the makings of a disaster unless Hanoi provided immediate help.

Laos held a central place in Hanoi's perspective at this juncture. Hanoi's strategy in Laos was a two-track one. On the one hand, Hanoi had encouraged NLHS participation in the coalition government, a policy that represented the switch from war against the French to the "new basis" (in the words of a Politburo resolution issued in September 1954) of relations between North Vietnam and the independent governments of Laos and Cambodia. The condition attached to this policy was that the NLHS would be able to extend indefinitely the temporary control over Sam Neua and Phong Saly that Hanoi's diplomacy had won at Geneva. Inside this liberated area Hanoi now secretly fostered the development of the "central organ" of the Laotian revolution,[4] which included a shadow government for all Laos under the direction of Pathet Lao leaders who were playing no part in the political scene in Vientiane. The armed forces at the command of this central revolutionary organ—the two Pathet Lao battalions scheduled to be integrated into the royal army—were still held in readiness for an alternative course of action if necessary.

On the other hand, Hanoi's need for a secure line of communication with the South was so great that Ho's government was not above appropriating, with a mixture of camouflage of purpose and brazenness of action, a strategically located piece of territory. Trails through the Annamite Chain guaranteed a security from observation that sea communication could not. Hanoi's leaders were not yet in a position to impose an agreement for cooperation on the Laotian government because they were still abiding by the public assurances they had given Souvanna Phouma about respecting the principle of noninterference in each other's internal affairs—the first track of Hanoi's policy toward Laos. Thus, use of trails through Laos, which would expose Hanoi to the risk of being accused of violating the Geneva Agreement, was inadvisable.

The North Vietnamese leaders, however, possessed a secret that would allow them to surmount this challenge. The secret concerned the piece of territory abutting the western extremity of the demilitarized zone agreed upon at Geneva. Because this territory lay west of the watershed in the Annamite Chain, it had been mapped by the French surveyors visiting this inhospitable region many years before as part of Laos's Savannakhet Province. But both Vietnamese governments claimed this territory on the basis of historical evidence—including tax receipts and forced labor registration cards—as part of Quang Tri Province.[5] As the French and Viet Minh experts had used a French map in drawing the demilitarized zone, they had shown its western extremity to be at the north-south line that the French took to be the border of Laos. But Hanoi's legal advisers claimed that the military experts had left the two zones of Vietnam *linked by a thin strip*. The practical import of this claim was that North Vietnam could move troops and arms through this strip without risk of being observed by the ICSC team in the demilitarized zone and without violating either the Geneva Agreement[6] or the sovereignty of Laos.

In late July and early August 1958, Hanoi published a series of articles under the title "Imperialist Schemes in Vietnam Against Peace and Reunification," which amounted to a staff study of U.S. aid to Diem's government. The decision to open the land route to South Vietnam must have been taken about this time. With the onset of the dry season in the dense forests of the Annamite Chain, Hanoi's troops set to work. North Vietnamese soldiers occupied several villages in the *tasseng* of Ban Kapai in Tchepone *muong* of Savannakhet Province. When Phoui's government received reports of the intruders flying North Vietnamese flags in these villages, he immediately protested to Hanoi. In the exchange of messages that followed, Pham Van Dong did not deny that North Vietnamese soldiers were occupying the area; he repeated the North Vietnamese claim that the area formed part of Huong Lap village, Huong Hoa district, Quang Tri Province, in accordance with historical evidence.

Phoui, however, took a grave view. Going before the National Assembly on January 12, 1959, he declared: "The situation is serious. Our eastern frontiers are seriously threatened." He asked for, and was granted, powers to rule by decree for one year. The North Vietnamese, for their part, remained in possession of Ban Kapai and counted on the likelihood that no deeper significance would be attached to the heated public exchanges over Huong Lap—an area remote from population centers and major roads and camouflaged by the triple canopy forest—than a dispute over conflicting border claims. Dong, indeed, had stonewalled past attempts by Souvanna Phouma to clear up outstanding border questions between their two countries, telling him their resolution would have to wait until Vietnam was reunified.

In that same month the Central Committee of the Vietnamese Workers party, at its Fifteenth Plenum, heard a first-hand report from Le Duan, the party's chief policymaker for the South who was to become party secretary general the following year, about conditions in South Vietnam and secretly decided to use armed force, combined with political action, to overthrow the Diem government. By the end of May, the North Vietnamese had secured complete control over Huong Lap, and the committee's Military Commission issued a resolution officially setting up Group 559. The mission given Group 559 was to create the first foot-travel route connecting the North with the South and to organize the transport of people (initially southerners regrouped to the North in 1954), weapons, and supplies to support the revolution in the South. The Ho Chi Minh Trail—which Dong much later called the key factor in the liberation of the South—had come into being.[7] Group 559 operated until the very end of the Indochina War; in February 1975, when the North Vietnamese were preparing for their last great offensive against South Vietnam, the headquarters of Group 559 was located west of Gio Linh on the Ben Hai River.[8] By that time, the North Vietnamese had completed a parallel road southward inside South Vietnam and were thus less dependent on the trails in Laos.

RESUMPTION OF THE CIVIL WAR

The special decree obtained by Phoui deprived the NLHS of any further role in the National Assembly. Hanoi's first-track strategy in Laos was set back even more when, at a press conference on February 11, Phoui announced that Laos had complied with all provisions of the Geneva Agreement; he thus defied Hanoi's position that Laos was bound by that agreement until the agreement on Vietnam had also been carried out.

Meanwhile, the crisis over the long-delayed attempt to integrate the two Pathet Lao battalions into the royal army came to a head. On May 11, the Second Pathet Lao Battalion refused integration at a ceremony on the Plain of Jars. The following day Phoui's government accused the NLHS of acting in collusion with North Vietnam and ordered the NLHS deputies in Vientiane placed under guard. A few days later it issued an ultimatum to the two battalions to accept integration within twenty-four hours. The First Battalion, which was quartered near Luang Prabang, accepted, apparently on orders from Souphanouvong, who was not anxious to see the NLHS lose all the gains it had made in terms of participation as a legal political party. With the Second Battalion, however, it was different story: On orders from the central organ in Sam Neua, this battalion decamped in the early hours of May 19 and "regained its revolutionary bases." In Vientiane, Souphanouvong and the other NLHS deputies were arrested.

North Vietnam now abandoned its first-track strategy entirely. Announcing that a situation of civil war existed in Laos, it threw its full support behind the Pathet Lao, whom it portrayed as fighting against a government in Vientiane completely under the domination of the United States. Fighting between the royal army and the Pathet Lao resumed sporadically on the Plain of Jars in July, and at the end of July Pathet Lao units, reinforced by North Vietnamese army cadres, launched concerted attacks against government outposts in Phong Saly, Sam Neua, and in the plateau country of southern Laos. Their object was obviously to consolidate the liberated areas in preparation for a protracted campaign of warfare against the Vientiane government.

In response to an appeal by Phoui, a United Nations mission visited Laos in September. From the documentation provided by the government and its visit to Sam Neua, the mission concluded that "certain of these hostile operations must have had centralized coordination;" however, hard evidence of North Vietnamese involvement was lacking at the time. But too much significance should not be attached to this because the attacking forces were operating from bases inside North Vietnam and consisted mostly of tribal minority personnel.

The North Vietnamese, in fact, were following a far different pattern than they had in their invasions of 1953 and 1954. Instead of sending entire military units across the border, they were attaching specialists to the Pathet Lao units they were training and equipping. Hanoi now officially admits that its people were present in the 1959 fighting.

In 1959, because of the revolutionary situation and missions in Laos, the Central Committee of the Vietnam Lao Dong Party and the Central Committee of the Laotian People's

Revolutionary Party, on the basis of close loyal cooperation
and solidarity in combat against the common enemy and
aggression, for the independence and freedom of the Vietnamese and Laotian people, and combining true patriotism
with pure proletarian internationalism, agreed to organize a
delegation of Vietnamese military specialists to work side-
by-side with the Military Commission and Supreme Command
of the Laotian People's Liberation Army.

In September 1959, Group 959 was set up and was assigned
the mission of serving as specialists for the Military Commission and Supreme Command of the Laotian People's
Liberation Army, and organizing the supplying of Vietnamese
materiel to the Laotian revolution and directly commanding
the Vietnamese volunteer units operating in Sam Neua, Xieng
Khouang, and Vientiane.[9]

The United States also responded by furnishing the hard-
pressed royal army with military equipment and training
teams in civilian dress, including 107 Special Forces troops.
In the midst of these disturbing events, King Sisavang Vong
died, after a reign of fifty-four years.

The expiration of the National Assembly's four-year
mandate on December 25 now provoked a constitutional crisis
of the sort that Laos, striving to imitate French parliamentary
procedure, could ill afford. Phoui wanted to make changes
in his cabinet but needed National Assembly's approval. To
convene the assembly, he first had to surrender his extraordinary powers, which he did. The changes he proposed were
not to the liking of the CDNI, however, so ambitious military
officers among this group (who held mostly minor cabinet
posts), led by Colonel Phoumi Nosavan, ordered their troops
to occupy government buildings. They also announced that
Phoui's resignation, which he had submitted to the king on
December 30 in the belief that his government's term would
be extended until it could organize new general elections,
had been accepted by the king and that a new caretaker
government would be set up. The king, however, had been
warned by the Western ambassadors in Vientiane—acting in
a rare display of solidarity—that to allow the CDNI to get
away with such a coup de force would damage Laos's con-

stitutional standing. The new government, therefore, did not consist of CDNI members, but was headed instead by Kou Abhay, a nonparty senior statesman.

The April 1960 general elections were no credit to the experiment of fostering democracy in a basically feudal kingdom. The CDNI was determined to ensure the victory of its supporters in revenge for the humiliation suffered in 1958. It tailored the qualification for candidates, gerrymandered electoral districts, and on election day bought votes with funds generously provided by helpful agents of the Central Intelligence Agency (CIA). In any case, the NLHS could not have mounted a serious challenge because its leaders were in jail in Vientiane or were in the bush. The following month Souphanouvong and the other imprisoned NLHS deputies escaped with the complicity of their prison guards. While they were making their way northward on foot, they heard astonishing news over the Vientiane radio, which caused them to decide to send back some of their party secretly on a mission to Vientiane.

KONG LE'S COUP D'ETAT

On the morning of August 9, 1960, the Vientiane radio began broadcasting communiqués that the "high command of the revolution" had taken into its hands all civil and military power. The communiqués were signed by Captain Kong Le, commanding officer of the Second Paratroop Battalion, a veteran unit of the fighting in Sam Neua in summer 1959 and of the preelection pacification campaign in southern Laos. The battalion had been scheduled to go out on operations that morning, but instead seized all public buildings and, against very little resistance, gained control over the capital of Laos.

As the new government of Prince Somsanith stepped up the pressure against the Pathet Lao in summer 1960, using U.S. arms and U.S. payroll funds, the young captain observed that the generals commanding the army (who now included Phoumi Nosavan) were enriching themselves in Vientiane while his soldiers were slogging along forest trails looking for the elusive Pathet Lao. The cost of the war was paid in Laotian blood, but the war itself was instigated by foreign paymasters and advisers. Realizing this truth made Kong Le a neutralist in the purest, most naive sense of the term. The politicians who styled themselves neutralists saw no objection to accepting foreign aid from either side to maintain a balance of influence; Kong Le did not want foreign aid or foreigners in the country, period. The way to peace, he believed, was to oust the Laotians who placed themselves at the beck and call of foreigners, and then the foreigners would have to leave. Kong Le remained loyal to this ideal; after circumstances forced him into an alliance with the Pathet Lao, he broke with them because he realized that they were serving their North Vietnamese masters in just the way that the royal army was serving the United States.

Plotting for the coup d'état went on actively through June and July in well-guarded secrecy. The only civilian Kong Le took into his confidence was Quinim Pholsena, leader of the Santiphab party, who had been defeated in the election. Quinim advised the paratroopers to get in touch with Souvanna Phouma who was again in Vientiane as chairman of the National Assembly, having returned from Paris to run in the election for deputy from Luang Prabang. Kong Le kept this bit of advice in mind: When the entire cabinet flew to Luang Prabang on August 8 to consult with the king on funeral arrangements for Sisavang Vong (whose body was to be cremated in a sandalwood bier in elaborate rites) he knew the hour had come.

Kong Le announced his aims: ending the civil war, resisting foreign pressures, removing foreign troops from the country, and suppressing those who were "making their harvest on the backs of the people." This simple program made him a popular figure among students and civil servants in Vientiane. As the ministers of Somsanith's government showed no sign of returning to Vientiane, a crowd of demonstrators marched on the National Assembly, which in a climactic meeting censured Somsanith by unanimous vote of the forty-one deputies present.

A deputation of the assembly carried the motion of no confidence to Luang Prabang next morning, together with a request that Souvanna Phouma be appointed prime minister. Prince Somsanith resigned that same day and returned to Vientiane accompanied by only one of his cabinet ministers, Ngon Sananikone. The others, together with several deputies of the assembly, had flown from Luang Prabang to Savannakhet immediately after receiving news of the coup. Led by General Phoumi, they proceeded to constitute a counter coup d'état committee.

After receiving the deputation in person, the king accepted Somsanith's resignation and allowed Souvanna Phouma to form a new government. Kong Le handed over the powers he had seized and declared his coup d'état at an end. Meanwhile from his base at Savannakhet, Phoumi proclaimed martial law. By denouncing the mutiny of the Second Paratroop Battalion and offering to pay the salaries of all civil servants and military personnel who remained loyal to him, Phoumi secured the allegiance of all military regional commanders except that for Vientiane. Consequently, when the documents for the investiture of the new government arrived in Luang Prabang, Phoumi prevented their being delivered to the king, arguing that martial law suspended government activity. Souvanna Phouma's government could not be invested and by a strict reading of the constitution could not take office, although its ministers had been sworn in at the Wat Sisaket in Vientiane in the traditional ceremony. As Hugh Toye noted, this meant that Phoumi's committee could allege claims to legality as well.

Phoumi now had formidable backing. His first action after leaving Luang Prabang had been to fly to Bangkok to consult Marshal Sarit Thanarat, the strong man of Thailand, whom Phoumi called uncle. Thailand gave him valuable support, notably by offering his forces safe passage over its territory, making possible an attack on Vientiane without hazarding Pathet Lao attacks in the Paksane bottleneck, and by cutting Vientiane's normal lines of supply through northeastern Thailand. But Phoumi's most important support came from the U.S. Central Intelligence Agency, which furnished him a radio transmitter and the services of Air America, a CIA contract company.

With John Foster Dulles's death, his brother Allen, the CIA director, was left to carry on the anti-Communist crusade, and in Laos Dulles's agents took full advantage of their official sanction and operated like an independent government with scant regard for the State Department and the U.S. ambassador. Phoumi's CIA contact, Jack Hazey, had his own reporting channels to Washington and assured Phoumi—whom he referred to as "our boy"—that he would supply an unending stream of dollars, materiel, and encouragement.

TWO RIVAL GOVERNMENTS

It was an awkward moment for Washington—a presidential election year. A U.S. decision to back Souvanna Phouma's new government, in effect turning the clock back to 1957, would have implied a conscious decision to reverse the policy of an entire administration. Sticking with the old policy was easier, even though it meant accepting the splitting up of the U.S.-trained army in Laos and an automatic weakening of the non-Communist forces in the country.

Souvanna Phouma faced a difficult choice. To refuse to attempt once again a negotiated settlement with the Pathet Lao would mean accepting the gamble of a military solution. And no one knew better that this move implied taking on the full weight of the North Vietnamese army. On the other hand, to accept the leadership offered to him, even in such dire circumstances, meant having to rely on the influence that North Vietnam's backers, the Soviet Union and China, could exert on the Laos situation.

Events now ran their course. Laos was placed for eighteen months in the same situation as Vietnam: It was controlled by two rival governments, each controlling part of the territory and each recognized by a different set of foreign powers. First, an attempt at reconciliation between Souvanna Phouma and Phoumi, under royal auspices in Luang Prabang at the end of August, came to nothing. Phoumi, who had been given the posts of deputy prime minister and minister of interior in Souvanna Phouma's government, did not assume his functions in Vientiane and returned to Savannakhet where, with the backing of Prince Boun Oum of Champassak, he proceeded to draw away a steady stream of civilian officials and military men from the government in Vientiane.

On August 24 the Pathet Lao radio had broadcast an appeal for support of Souvanna Phouma and on September 19 announced that Pathet Lao troops had been ordered to avoid clashes with troops loyal to him. On September 26, Pathet Lao troops, "in coordination with the Vietnamese volunteer troops,"[10] reoccupied Sam Neua town, forcing the royal garrison there, whose commander had hesitated to join Souvanna Phouma, to flee; the Pathet Lao were never again to leave Sam Neua.

When Souvanna Phouma formally opened talks with Pathet Lao emissaries in Vientiane in mid-October, the United States made known its displeasure by suspending the cash-grant aid program that was used to pay military salaries. A few days later, J. Graham Parsons—who, although having failed as ambassador to prevent the coalition of 1957, had been named to succeed Walter S. Robertson as the State Department's chief Far Eastern policymaker—returned to Vientiane to haunt Souvanna Phouma by demanding that the negotiations with the Pathet Lao be broken off. Parsons—whom Souvanna Phouma later described as having "understood nothing about Asia and nothing about Laos"—failed in his mission and the talks proceeded.

U.S. ambassador Winthrop Brown was sympathetic toward Souvanna Phouma but found no one in Washington to listen to him. He was instructed to obtain Souvanna Phouma's assent to continued provision of military aid to Phoumi in Savannakhet in return for a resumption of the cash-grant program. Souvanna Phouma agreed, but on one condition: Military aid to Phoumi was to be used exclusively for the defense of the country and not against Kong Le's forces. However, no commitment was made by Phoumi on this point, and when he used U.S. military aid to capture Vientiane in December, Souvanna Phouma accused the United States of double-crossing him and his government. Meanwhile,

The neutralists: Prince Souvanna Phouma (left) and Captain Kong Le.
(Photos in author's collection)

Souvanna Phouma invited the Soviets to establish an embassy
in Vientiane and received promises of Soviet aid in badly
needed supplies, especially petroleum, to the blockaded capital.
A Soviet airlift from Hanoi to Vientiane was started in
December.

After the garrison in Luang Prabang switched to Phoumi's
side, Souvanna Phouma declared that he would not be bound
by decisions made by the king, if the king were not a free
agent. In mid-November he flew to Sam Neua for a meeting
with Souphanouvong, who had just completed his long trek
from Vientiane. The two agreed in principle on the formation
of a new coalition government.

But by now Phoumi's troops were rapidly approaching
Vientiane. A number of hit-and-run raids had already been
staged on the capital, and Kong Le's defenders were dug in
for the main assault. In early December, Phoumi's U.S.-
supplied howitzers began shelling the capital. In the ensuing
battle, between seven and eight hundred persons, mainly
civilians, were killed, and Kong Le's forces began their withdrawal up the Luang Prabang road. Seeing the battle coming,
Souvanna Phouma with most of his ministers flew off to

Phnom Penh. He left behind his information minister, Quinim Pholsena, who secretly flew to Hanoi aboard a Soviet transport plane. There he concluded a deal: In exchange for military supplies to be delivered to Kong Le's troops, Souvanna Phouma's government agreed to a formal alliance between Kong Le and the Pathet Lao.

Even before his entry into the capital at the head of his victorious forces, Phoumi had had the thirty-eight National Assembly deputies in Savannakhet pass a censure motion against Souvanna Phouma's government. Royal ordinances that dismissed this last and gave provisional powers to the Savannakhet group were signed by the king on December 12. The head of the new provisional government was Prince Boun Oum of Champassak. Although the United States, Thailand, Britain, and France switched their recognition to this government, India, the Soviet Union, and China continued to recognize Souvanna Phouma's government, which had not resigned before flying into exile.

In Phnom Penh, Souvanna Phouma was visited by Quinim and Phoumi Vongvichit, who dissuaded him from giving up politics and retiring to France. They assured him that, if he were not willing to return to Laos with them, he would at least have a skeleton government in place in Khang Khay, where Kong Le had set up his headquarters, and he could return there later. Henceforth, Souvanna Phouma maintained that the king and the National Assembly had acted under duress, and thus illegally, in investing the Boun Oum government. There now were two "legal" governments in Laos.

TWO RIVAL ARMIES

From the start of the new year, while Kong Le refitted his troops with Soviet weapons arriving on the Plain of Jars by road and airlift (a British observer there in February reported that his overwhelming impression was that of massive military assistance), the Pathet Lao, powerfully backed by North Vietnam's Group 959, extended the liberated area to include much of five provinces. One after another Phoumi's

garrisons abandoned their positions to the Pathet Lao and
the "volunteer" Vietnamese troops: Nam Bac and Ban Ban
(January 4), Tha Vieng (January 12), Vang Vieng and Tha
Thom (January 18), Moung Hiem (January 29), Pa Thi (January
31), Sala Phou Khoun (March 7), Kam Keut-Lak Sao-Nape
(March 11), and Pha Tang (March 19).[11]

As Phoumi's military situation worsened, the United
States stepped up its assistance, furnishing Harvard trainer
aircraft fitted with bomb racks and also providing advisers
on the ground. These last, special forces known as White
Star teams attached to royal army units in the field, now
operated under a full-scale Military Assistance Advisory Group
(MAAG) and numbered four hundred. They helped make up
for often incompetent leadership in the field; Phoumi's army
had swelled to more than forty thousand, but was short of
officers.

The strategic initiative lay with the North Vietnamese
leaders, whose military command knew how to make the
best use of well-disciplined veteran combat troops in attacks
alongside the Pathet Lao at places and times of their own
choosing. This "people's army" was no ragtag peasant militia,
but a regular army hardened in the long struggle against the
French over the same terrain. Even so, it did pay a price:
The North Vietnamese estimated their casualties in the fighting
in Laos from February to June 1961 at seven hundred killed
or wounded.[12] Many of these casualties were inflicted by the
Hmong tribespeople who inhabited the mountainous region
between the Plain of Jars and the Mekong valley. These
tribespeople were being recruited, trained, and formed into
irregular units that operated in similar fashion to the Pathet
Lao, under the leadership of Vang Pao, a former French army
sergeant.

During April, a strong attack by Kong Le's paratroopers
and Pathet Lao troops cut the road to Luang Prabang in the
Vang Vieng region, sending Phoumi's troops reeling back to
the Nam Lik and provoking renewed diplomatic activity. A
tenuous cease-fire went into effect from May 3, and negotiations began between the opposing sides, under the good
offices of the ICSC, which was reactivated and dispatched
to Laos by the Geneva cochairmen. The negotiations took

place first on the front line at the Nam Lik crossing, then in the village schoolhouse at Ban Namone inside Pathet Lao–controlled territory. Three delegations—one each representing the Pathet Lao, the Phoumists, and Souvanna Phouma (who had returned from his self-imposed exile and taken up residence at Khang Khay)—sat around a U-shaped table under the Laotian flag.

After seven years, the United States had finally accepted the principle of a coalition government in Laos—a policy change brought about by President John F. Kennedy. Kennedy concluded that supporting a government bent on achieving a military victory over the Pathet Lao was not realistic: the Phoumists were no match for those who had gone from being rebels to allies of a purportedly legal government and who were more strongly backed by North Vietnam than ever before. The Bay of Pigs fiasco had made Kennedy skeptical of the chances of success of the Phoumists without direct U.S. military intervention, and he was leary of the latter.

Kennedy's change of policy was politically courageous. Although he enlisted British Prime Minister Harold Macmillan to persuade Eisenhower not to encourage talk of a military solution in Laos, in a meeting with the former president two weeks later he confessed that the loss of Laos to the Communists would also imperil Thailand, thereby accepting the domino theory.[13] Kennedy knew he was vulnerable at home to the charge of appeasement. The new policy saw the coalition as a way of avoiding U.S. intervention and at the same time of separating the Pathet Lao from North Vietnam. The man responsible for executing this policy, Ambassador Averell Harriman, against all odds succeeded in winning back the confidence of Souvanna Phouma. Harriman's most difficult moments were not with Souvanna Phouma but with Phoumi, who still assumed that his friends in the CIA would be able to subvert the U.S. overtures to Souvanna Phouma.

THE 1961–1962 GENEVA CONFERENCE

The talks at Ban Namone were still in progress when the foreign ministers of the nations that attended the 1954 Geneva Conference convened there again on May 16 to take

Three princes' meeting, Ban Hin Heup, October 1961. Left to right: Prince Boun Oum of Champassak, Prince Souvanna Phouma, Prince Souphan-ouvong, and General Phoumi Nosavan. (Photo in author's collection)

up the problem of Laos, in accordance with a proposal put forward by Prince Norodom Sihanouk of Cambodia. This time, however, the Pathet Lao were seated as equals with the delegations from Souvanna Phouma's and Boun Oum's governments.

In spite of a discussion of Laos between President Kennedy and Soviet Premier Nikita Khrushchev in Vienna in June 1961 and further meetings of the three parties to the conflict, including one among the three princes in Zurich that same month, little progress was made toward setting up the coalition already agreed upon in principle. Another three princes' meeting in Vientiane in December, called to consider an appeal from the ministers in Geneva to the Laotian parties to form a unified government, broke up in disarray after Boun Oum and Phoumi adopted a hard line on the division of cabinet seats, thereby setting back what little progress had been made.

In May 1962, taking advantage of the respite he had won, Phoumi launched his biggest gamble. Obviously intent on involving U.S. military forces in Laos, he engineered a set-piece battle between his troops and the Pathet Lao–North Vietnamese forces over the provincial capital of Nam Tha in northwestern Laos. Overcome by an assault by the latter, the Phoumist troops abandoned their heavy weapons and fled pell-mell down the trail to the Mekong, which they crossed in large numbers to safety in Thailand. Phoumi, calculating that his deliberately exaggerated estimates of the attacking force would bring him U.S. help, succeeded in panicking the Thai, who disarmed the fleeing troops. Kennedy, however, kept his cool. He had previously ordered the upgrading of facilities at a number of airfields in northeastern Thailand. Now he ordered U.S. combat units from Okinawa to the same area to take up positions "because of recent attacks in Laos by Communist forces, the subsequent movement of Communist military units toward the border of Thailand." But he went no further. Phoumi had no recourse but to bow to Harriman's ultimatum—which was enforced by a cutoff of U.S. aid—and to join the tripartite coalition.

Final agreement was hammered out in talks among the three princes on the Plain of Jars from June 7 to 12. The provisional government of national union was to consist of seven of Souvanna Phouma's neutralists, four Phoumists, four NLHS members, and four so-called right-wing neutralists, people who had remained in Vientiane without commitment to Phoumi. In Geneva on June 23, a unified Laotian delegation participated in the signing by fourteen countries of an international agreement neutralizing Laos.

NOTES

1. Anthony Eden, minuting the Foreign Office from Geneva, described Walter S. Robertson, the State Department's top official for Far Eastern affairs, as a person "whose approach to these questions is so emotional as to be impervious to argument or indeed facts." (Anthony Eden, *Full Circle: The Memoirs of Anthony Eden*, Boston: Houghton Mifflin Co., 1960, p. 126.)

2. *North Vietnam* is used here as a term of convenience reflecting the post-1954 geographical reality. Ho's government recognized no such state and continued after the partition to regard

itself as the sole legitimate government of all Vietnam. The first article of the constitution of the Democratic Republic of Vietnam adopted in 1960 proclaimed: "Vietnam is an integral whole encompassing both the North and the South and is indivisible."

3. U.S. Department of State, *Foreign Relations of the United States 1952–1954*, vol. 16, *The Geneva Conference* (Washington: Government Printing Office, 1981), p. 1226.

4. *Cuoc Khang Chien Chong My Cuu Nuoc 1954–1975: Nhung Su Kien Quan Su* [The Anti-U.S. Resistance War for National Salvation 1954–1975: Military Events] (Hanoi: War Experiences Recapitulation Committee of the High-Level Military Institute, People's Army Publishing House, 1980), p. 14.

5. This border area had historically paid tribute to both Annam and Vieng Chan to preserve the peace. The detailed history of the area together with a map can be found in Arthur J. Dommen, *Conflict in Laos: The Politics of Neutralization*, rev. ed. (New York: Praeger Publishers, 1971), pp. 338–351.

The demilitarized zone was delimited subsequent to the Geneva Conference by French and Viet Minh experts of the Trung Gia Military Commission, acting under the instruction that the provisional military demarcation line was to run along the parallel of the village of Bo Ho Su "to the Laos–Viet Nam frontier." (See United Kingdom, Cmd. 9239, *Further Documents Relating to the Discussion of Indo-China at the Geneva Conference, June 16–July 21, 1954*, Misc. no. 20, 1954, "Annex to the Agreement on the Cessation of Hostilities in Viet Nam" [London: HMSO, 1959] p. 39.) As the French map of Indochina at 1/100,000 scale used in this delimitation showed the Laos-Vietnam border to be east of the position later claimed by Hanoi, the western extremity of the demilitarized zone coincided with this border. The portions of this map (sheets 119-E and 119-W) showing the position of the demilitarized zone are reprinted in U.S. Department of State, Office of the Geographer, International Boundary Study no. 19, *Viet-Nam "Demarcation Line,"* Washington, D.C., September 10, 1962.

6. Article 6 of the Agreement on Cessation of Hostilities in Vietnam read: "No person, military or civilian, shall be permitted to cross the provisional military demarcation line unless specifically authorized to do so by the Joint Commission."

7. Interview on "Vietnam: A Television History," transcript no. 106, p. 15.

8. General Van Tien Dung, *Our Great Spring Victory* (New York: Monthly Review Press, 1977), p. 38.

9. *Cuoc Khang,* pp. 54–55.

10. Ibid., p. 72.

11. Ibid., p. 77.

12. Marek Thee, *Notes of a Witness: Laos and the Second Indochinese War* (New York: Random House, 1973), p. 129.

13. On September 9, 1963, Kennedy was asked in a television interview whether he subscribed to the domino theory. "I believe it," he replied.

5

The Final Years of the Kingdom (1962–1975)

The widely held hope that formation of the second coalition government in Laos's modern history and international guarantees of Laos's neutrality would ease the crisis was soon dashed. Warfare resumed on a large scale, with increasing outside intervention, and the new coalition survived in practice barely as long as the first, though it existed in name for another decade. The reasons for this turn of events lay in developments elsewhere in Indochina.

BEHIND THE FIGHTING

For the North Vietnamese, the alliance between the Pathet Lao and Souvanna Phouma's government from December 1960 onward provided notable tactical advantages. First, the alliance was an expedient that provided diplomatic cover for their involvement on the ground in Laos. Since they had reasons for such involvement beyond the interests of the revolution in Laos, this cover represented an important gain. Second, the alliance furnished the pretext for deliveries of Soviet supplies to the Pathet Lao and Kong Le, allowing the forces of the former to upgrade their military capability significantly. Third, the alliance provided the NLHS with a prototype of a coalition government in operation. The NLHS and the neutralists, represented at the top by Souphanouvong and Souvanna Phouma, made all decisions jointly, although such decisions were implemented in the latter's name. Below the central government level, the coalition principle was also applied: Coalition provincial administrations existed in Sam Neua, Phong Saly, Xieng Khouang, and Vientiane provinces (the last having its seat at Vang Vieng). Below that level, coalition administration extended down to the district level, although most districts were controlled by the Pathet Lao forces rather than Kong Le's. At the village level, full authority was in the hands of the NLHS, who made a practice of replacing village headpersons with their own cadres as soon as their forces took control of an area. Although the NLHS paid lip service to the coalition at the top, its cadres were able to extend their control to almost all areas claiming allegiance to Souvanna Phouma; in fact, the latter's infrequent attempts to send his own people to run things were resisted by force of arms.

The NLHS thus proved the effectiveness of a revolutionary movement that owed its primary loyalty to a central directorate completely outside the bourgeois political setup and uniquely able, on the basis of accurate political and military intelligence, to weigh the balance of forces and the possibilities for further action on behalf of the revolution. Compliance with orders issued from the central directorate was ensured by the threat of military reprisal.

Much has been made of the sheer weight of military power brought to bear by the United States in Laos between 1962 and 1973. But military power, no matter how great, that is not directed to the attainment of specific political goals loses much of its value in a political-military struggle such as that in Laos. The United States stood for the survival of the Kingdom of Laos and of its elected government, threatened by subversion from within and coercion from without. This honorable goal was largely devalued by the corrupt methods used in the 1960 elections to pack the National Assembly with right-wing supporters and by the ambition and greed of people like General Phoumi who placed personal gain above the national interest. In many ways, the contest was unequal from the start: Hanoi exercised full control over its instruments of power, both military and political, whereas the United States only had control over its military power.

This difference presupposes another, more fundamental difference in the relations between Hanoi and Washington and their Laotian clients. Hanoi maintained control over the NLHS through its control over the central directorate (described in Chapter 6); Washington attempted to work through the traditional structures of governance of a largely feudal society.

In June 1961 a privileged foreign visitor to the central directorate of the Indochinese revolutions in Hanoi had a first-hand glimpse that gives substance to what otherwise would be only supposition about the pattern of decisionmaking at that crucial time. This visitor had conversations with all the principals involved in directing moves in Laos, beginning with Politburo member Pham Hung; Deputy Foreign Minister Hoang Van Tien; the chief of the Laos desk in the Central Committee of the Vietnamese Workers party, Nguyen Chinh Giao; his close associate, Tran Chi Hien; and department chief in the Foreign Ministry Dao Viet Dinh. These conversations made it clear that with respect to Laos the North Vietnamese were motivated not so much by the general international situation as by the situation on the ground.

The logic of this ingrained parochialism for the leaders in Hanoi dictated that their actions were susceptible to influence less from the advice of their allies—the Soviets and the Chinese—than from their ever-changing and ever-attuned perceptions of what their adversaries—the Americans, the South Vietnamese, the Thai, and the Phoumists—were doing. Thus, they felt that such international events as the Vienna meeting between Kennedy and Soviet Premier Khrushchev did not change actual priorities or the long-range appraisal of events. And the provisions of the 1962 Geneva Agreement on Laos applied only to international commitments to respect Laos's neutrality and did not give license to other powers to meddle in Laos's internal affairs.[1] Only Hanoi had the right to interfere, since the revolution in Laos was an internal affair and one that concerned Hanoi directly by virtue of the secret alliance among the revolutionary parties in the three Indochinese countries. Neutralization of Laos thus implied U.S. withdrawal, leaving the Pathet Lao, pliable instruments in the hands of the Vietnamese Communists, to carry on the revolution.

In summer 1961, North Vietnamese forces and their Pathet Lao allies were winning on all fronts in Laos. But the North Vietnamese leaders remained deeply mistrustful of the United States: U.S. actions on the ground in Laos did not seem to bear out Kennedy's public professions about supporting a neutral Laos under a coalition government. They felt that in Laos, as in South Vietnam, the true U.S. intention was to destroy the revolutionary forces. They concluded that, as long as the United States insisted on maintaining a military presence in any corner of the Indochinese Peninsula, no negotiated compromise could last long; only effective military and political assets had any value.[2]

In geopolitical terms, this global view meant that the Pathet Lao had to keep control of their actual holdings, even if a tripartite coalition government were formed, to preserve their alliance with the neutralists, and to work continuously for conditions that would enhance their own influence with the people. Especially menacing were U.S. attempts from bases in South Vietnam and Thailand to prevent the Pathet Lao and their North Vietnamese allies from controlling more and more of Laos's territory. In particular, the North Vietnamese saw in efforts by Diem's government and the Phoumists to secure Route 9 in southern Laos a strategic U.S. design to link the border of Thailand at Savannakhet with the South Vietnamese coast at Da Nang. This design would imperil the Ho Chi Minh Trail, which was assuming ever greater importance in Hanoi's own strategic planning.

In summer 1961, therefore, the North Vietnamese saw events in Laos as moving not toward peace, but toward war. When it became known in Moscow, this view provoked "stupefaction and dismay."[3] The Soviets were hoping to defuse the Laos crisis by agreement with the United States, and their first reaction was that the North Vietnamese must have formed such a view under the pernicious influence of the Chinese, with whom the Soviets were having their first difficulties. This reaction was as far off the mark as the U.S. tendency to see China's hand behind every Communist advance in Indochina.

In September, the Soviets sent a memorandum to the Vietnamese Workers party disagreeing with Hanoi's policy in Laos, criticizing the conditions that the NLHS was attaching to participation in a future coalition government, and citing unwillingness to name top party leaders to ministerial posts.[4] The memorandum also expressed dissatisfaction with Hanoi's allocation of Soviet aid in Laos, saying that the neutralists were not receiving a fair share, which weakened the alliance. Hanoi actually was not only diverting Soviet supplies from the neutralists to the Pathet Lao (a fact that surfaced in complaints by Kong Le), but was also sending some of these supplies, such as bulldozers, farther to the south to construct roads through Laos to South Vietnam.

Once the 1962 Geneva Agreement had been signed, the Soviets were quick to halt their airlift from Hanoi to Tchepone, which the Pathet Lao had seized just before the cease-fire went into effect. In spite of his famous speech in January 1961 about supporting "wars of national liberation," Khrushchev was anxious not to provoke the United States by furnishing material assistance to the North Vietnamese for a conquest of South Vietnam by force of arms. The Soviets turned their airlift planes over to Souvanna Phouma's new government in Vientiane.

Hanoi's certainty about the move toward war in Laos was reinforced by the mission of General Maxwell Taylor, Kennedy's special emissary, to Saigon in October 1961. Diem's government was increasingly threatened by Communist guerrillas, and Kennedy, ever mindful of the domino theory, was about to step up the U.S. commitment to Diem. A Phoumist offensive in southern Laos at just this time, rumors that South Vietnamese forces were to be used across the border of Laos to cut infiltration routes, reinforced Hanoi's suspicions still further. The offensive in southern Laos momentarily threatened an important new road that the North Vietnamese had built with the onset of the dry season from Sa Ang on Route 12 down to Tchepone, a hub of the Ho Chi Minh Trail.

The conversion of the MAAG in Saigon to a full-scale Military Assistance Command Vietnam (MACV) in February 1962 was soon followed by a quickened pace of military supplies to Diem, including large numbers of helicopters and more U.S. advisers. In 1962, the Communist apparatus in South Vietnam, now operating under the umbrella of the South Vietnam National Liberation Front (NLF), patterned on the NLHS and the Viet Minh, took a good deal of punishment before it learned to cope with the new tactics. The NLF, in an important statement in March at the conclusion of its first congress, appealed for setting up a coalition government in Saigon. At the same time, North Vietnamese negotiators at the Geneva conference began sounding out dissident South Vietnamese politicians about participating in such a government and talking about convening a new Geneva conference on South Vietnam. These initiatives, however, met with no response in Saigon or Washington, and Hanoi soon returned to the idea of fighting the war on the battlefield.

THE SECOND COALITION

During a private talk with Pham Van Dong on a visit to Hanoi June 16–17, immediately following the Plain of Jars agreement on a coalition government, Souvanna Phouma raised the issues foremost in his mind about North Vietnam's intentions: withdrawal of North Vietnamese military personnel from Laos and the Ho Chi Minh Trail. On the first, Dong was reassuring: His government was interested in easing Souvanna Phouma's tasks and would therefore comply with any demands put forward by the Laotian government. On the second, Souvanna Phouma received far less reassurance: Dong said that the war unleashed by the United States in South Vietnam and southern Laos flowed naturally across the border. He added that the trails through Laos served only for contacts and movements of cadres, not for military units. His government, he said, did not wish to create unnecessary difficulties for Laos, and the blame lay with the United States, which should return to the Vietnam settlement provided in the 1954 agreement. His government would continue to assist its brothers in the South. This conversation between the two men—in which Dong admitted for the first time the existence of the trails through Laos although obviously lying about their purpose—was a very frank exchange.

After the signing of the 1962 Geneva Agreement, Souvanna Phouma went to Washington, where he had conversations with President Kennedy and his top advisers. He found the Americans preoccupied with the situation in South Vietnam. Laos, in their view, was a problem whose solution lay with the U.S.-Soviet understanding reached at Vienna in 1961. Kennedy assured the prince that his administration backed the neutralist policies of the coalition government and no longer those of the former Boun Oum government. Nevertheless, important issues remained to be resolved, namely, the integration of the armed forces in Laos, the conduct of future elections, and the effectiveness of the ICSC, especially with regard to infiltration to South Vietnam. Kennedy suggested that, in order to assure peace in Laos, the United States would maintain a certain degree of armed strength in neighboring countries. The U.S. view of the necessary conditions for the neutralization of Laos was put most forcefully by Secretary of Defense Robert McNamara, who told Souvanna Phouma that, in accordance with the protocol to the Geneva Agreement, Laotian territory should not be used for infiltration from North to South Vietnam. The infiltration must stop, he said, and the political independence in Southeast Asia would not be achieved unless the infiltration was halted. This statement, resting on the classic European position that a neutral state does not give sanctuary to foreign troops, expressed a very different viewpoint on the position of Laos from that held in Hanoi.

North Vietnam's intentions with respect to Laos became clearer in August when large truck convoys were detected by U.S. reconnaissance missions from bases in Thailand. These missions were necessary because the intensity of antiaircraft fire around the Plain of Jars had made it impossible to rely on slow, propellor-driven planes of the royal Laotian air force. The North Vietnamese were moving in what appeared to analysts to be a permanent military presence in Laos. But

Kennedy—who was preoccupied with puzzling out the significance of Soviet hardware shipments to Fidel Castro's Cuba—did not react to the intelligence from Laos when he received it. Thus the United States forfeited the opportunity to make a serious issue of this blatant violation of Article 4 of the 1962 protocol, which stipulated as follows: "The introduction of foreign regular and irregular troops, foreign paramilitary formations, and foreign military personnel into Laos is prohibited."

With respect to the withdrawal of foreign military personnel within seventy-five days as stipulated in Article 2 of the protocol, North Vietnam's leaders delayed a decision until almost the final day, suspecting that the United States would not withdraw its MAAG. Actually, the MAAG was withdrawn on schedule under ICSC verification, as provided for in the protocol. Finally, on October 5, two days before the deadline, Dong sent a personal message to Souvanna Phouma through the newly opened North Vietnamese Embassy in Vientiane, informing him that the Politburo had made the decision to withdraw all Vietnamese personnel without exception, *conditional* on the behavior of the United States and the rightist faction.⁴

Kennedy's policy in Laos was based on neutralization and therefore implied acceptance of the prohibition in the Geneva protocol against foreign military personnel. However, since the success of U.S. efforts to help Diem depended on cutting the trails through Laos on which the NLF guerrillas depended, Kennedy was prepared to authorize actions that could be taken without violating the protocol. The United States therefore continued its reconnaissance flights, resumed delivery of military supplies to the rightist faction, and established a disguised military aid mission called the Requirements Office staffed by retired military personnel in civilian clothes working under cover of the economic aid mission in Vientiane. Although such U.S. actions were taken with Souvanna Phouma's knowledge (and in the case of military supplies, at his request), they had not been voted upon by the tripartite coalition, where they would certainly have been vetoed by the NLHS. The North Vietnamese thus had a plausible excuse in Dong's letter not to abide by Article 2. Faced with this Hobson's choice, Souvanna Phouma, knowing full well the military threat posed by the North Vietnamese, chose to rely on the security measures Kennedy offered him. Thus, U.S. involvement in Laos grew, and the North Vietnamese troops remained.

The refusal of the Pathet Lao–North Vietnamese to allow inspection teams of the ICSC into the liberated area, an obligation clearly assumed by the NLHS under articles 11, 12, and 16 of the protocol, made it particularly difficult for Souvanna Phouma to avoid siding more and more with the rightist faction in the coalition. (The NLHS was still obstructing efforts to station an inspection team on the Plain of Jars in April 1963 at the moment serious fighting broke out there.) The failure of the ICSC machinery at this critical point had dire consequences for restraining the North Vietnamese from further expanding the liberated area and from using Laos for secure passage of their troops and supplies into South Vietnam.

The chronology of events during this period makes it fairly clear that North Vietnam's leaders never had any intention of withdrawing their troops and advisers from Laos following signature of the 1962 agreement. At the end of August, an estimated ten thousand North Vietnamese military personnel were in Laos, including the members of Group 559 along the trail, the advisers of Group 959, and almost a dozen frontier guard battalions posted on the passes across the Annamite Chain. Souvanna Phouma had few illusions about North Vietnamese intentions; he had dealt with their leaders for too long. He gambled on his good personal relations with the leaders of the major foreign powers involved in Laos—the United States, France, Britain, India, the Soviet Union, and China—to dissuade the Laos factions, both on the Left and on the Right, from attempting to upset the balance of forces along the unpoliced cease-fire line. All these powers maintained embassies in Vientiane after 1962, and the normal rounds of diplomatic life in the capital camouflaged the war that was tearing the country apart, spreading death and destruction and creating refugees by the hundreds of thousands. The Soviets staffed their embassy mainly with specialists on the United States.

The North Vietnamese steeled themselves for a hard campaign against the Americans along the Ho Chi Minh Trail. They must have realized that Kennedy, having authorized covert means to protect Souvanna Phouma's government, would not hesitate to authorize bombing attacks against the trail complex from bases in South Vietnam and Thailand and from carriers at sea in an effort to interrupt the movement of supplies southward. In spite of North Vietnamese propaganda about U.S. violations of the Geneva protocol, these bombing raids did not strictly infringe on the prohibition against the introduction of foreign military personnel. To Pathet Lao cadres who inquired what the North Vietnamese soldiers were doing in Laos after Geneva, they replied that they were only borrowing the trail until the war was over. U.S. bombing of the trail did not begin until Kennedy's successor, Lyndon B. Johnson, had assumed the burden of the war in Indochina, and thereafter Souvanna Phouma spoke of the bombing as involving only North Vietnam and the United States—a situation that did not much concern the rest of Laos.

By 1962, the Soviets were rapidly withdrawing their support from the North Vietnamese in Laos and encouraging the NLHS to place its trust in Souvanna Phouma. They terminated their airlift between Vietnam and Laos and, in response to Souvanna Phouma's urgent requests to both the Soviet Union and the United States for aircraft to resupply royal army outposts isolated behind Pathet Lao lines, placed their planes at the disposal of the Vientiane government for an interim period. The United States responded by providing Air America planes and crews under contract to the Laotian Ministry of Public Works and Transport. The Soviets' abrupt termination of their airlift angered Hanoi and became a factor in Hanoi's development of closer ties to China in this period.

Under the stresses and strains to which it was subjected, the coalition government in Laos, put together amid such high hopes, soon began to unravel. The year 1962 was not yet over when antiaircraft gunners on the Plain of Jars

belonging to a dissident faction of neutralists heavily indoc-
trinated by the Pathet Lao shot down an Air America C-123
flying supplies to Kong Le. NLHS efforts to subvert Kong
Le's troops were backed up by assassination of some of the
little captain's (now general's) most trusted officers. By spring
1963, when open warfare resumed on the plain, Kong Le
had to retreat to more defensible positions on the plain's
western edge. On April 1, the coalition's foreign minister,
Quinim Pholsena, was assassinated in Vientiane. The NLHS
ministers, claiming lack of security, immediately departed for
the liberated area. Souvanna Phouma held vacant their port-
folios, but the empty chairs at weekly cabinet meetings bespoke
the unreality of the coalition.

In January 1964, following a preliminary round of talks
among representatives of the three factions on the Plain of
Jars, Souvanna Phouma and Souphanouvong met in Sam
Neua and reaffirmed their support for the principle of coalition.
But the continued fighting, accompanied by the usual con-
tradictory charges of foreign intervention, made effective
reconstitution of the government impossible. A few days
afterward, the Pathet Lao–North Vietnamese opened their
dry season campaign in central Laos and against Kong Le's
remaining positions on the plain. A pessimistic Souvanna
Phouma left for visits to Hanoi and Peking in early April,
again with the issue of North Vietnamese troops uppermost
in his mind. General Giap told Souvanna Phouma that Hanoi
would not tolerate troops other than the Pathet Lao on the
Plain of Jars. In these circumstances, a new tripartite meeting
among Souvanna Phouma, Souphanouvong, and Phoumi on
April 17 failed to produce any result, and on his return to
Vientiane, Souvanna Phouma announced his intention of
resigning.

The prime minister's announcement precipitated action
on the rightist side, where discontent had been brewing for
some time. Two rightist generals staged a coup attempt on
April 19 and arrested Souvanna Phouma. One of them, the
commander of the Vientiane military region, had been trying
to gain control over Kong Le's garrison at Vang Vieng, which
was in his territory but which had been placed under a

special command by Souvanna Phouma as defense minister. Relations between the rightist generals and Phoumi had been tense, and a good deal of personal rivalry was involved.

The coup attempt broke down, however, when U.S. Ambassador Leonard Unger reaffirmed support for the coalition and urged Phoumi to act to restore order in the armed forces. Souvanna Phouma, released from arrest, pledged to merge the rightist and centrist armed forces. However, he became increasingly identified with the rightist faction (particularly after Phoumi fled to Thailand in February 1965 following a renewed outbreak of infighting among the generals). Another consequence of the coup attempt was to make the regional military commanders virtual warlords in their own domains.

ESCALATION

Meanwhile, in March the United States, responding to the renewed fighting on the plain, had moved the first squadron of fighter-bombers into position at an air base in Thailand as a precautionary move and on May 21 announced that U.S. reconnaissance jets were flying over Laos at Souvanna Phouma's request to gather information about Communist troop dispositions. After the loss of two such planes to antiaircraft fire, Souvanna Phouma gave his verbal assent to Ambassador Unger for the reconnaissance flights to be accompanied by armed escorts. Souvanna Phouma forwarded to the ICSC aerial photographs of North Vietnamese troop convoys in the Mu Gia Pass headed for Laos.

The onset of the dry season in October saw the largest round of escalation and counterescalation in the Ho Chi Minh Trail area to date. The trail network, which had originally accommodated files of people pushing bicycles laden with sacks and crates, was enlarged by the North Vietnamese into roads capable of handling truck convoys and tanks. This work allowed them to reequip all Communist main-force units in South Vietnam with the 7.62-millimeter weapons system by the early weeks of 1965 and to send the first regular North Vietnamese Army regiments into the South in mid-1965. The

United States began systematic bombing of the trail complex in January 1965 from bases in Thailand.

The escalation of the war coincided with the reengagement of the post-Khrushchev Soviet leadership with North Vietnam—symbolized by the visit to Hanoi of Premier Aleksei Kosygin in February 1965—whereas Laos continued to be an area of U.S.-Soviet understanding. The escalation of the fighting had made the U.S. policy dilemma in Laos more complex. The first phase of Kennedy's policy had been successfully implemented: the winning back of Souvanna Phouma from the arms of the Pathet Lao where Dulles's confrontation policy had driven him. The second phase, however—separating the Pathet Lao from the North Vietnamese—proved problematical. With heavy fighting going on between the Pathet Lao and the rightists, the former simply were not in a position to forsake Hanoi's embrace as they might have been tempted to do in peacetime.

Kennedy's successors, however, continued the reliance on the U.S.-Soviet understanding about Laos. This understanding meant that the United States would operate by covert means in Laos, thereby not confronting the Soviet Union with open violations of the 1962 agreement that would compel the Soviets to take action to maintain their credibility with Hanoi. The United States paid a heavy price for this big-power duplicity. In spite of the legitimacy of its actions in Laos on behalf of an independent and sovereign government defending itself against foreign aggression, the secrecy that shrouded these actions (the Defense Department, for instance, went to the length of describing military personnel lost in Laos as missing in action "in Southeast Asia") led to an outcry in Congress that the United States was engaged in a secret, and by implication illegitimate, war in Laos. By contrast, the North Vietnamese leadership, which operated with a secrecy that was routine for totalitarian regimes, faced no such problem.

President Johnson allowed the ambassadorial-level talks in Warsaw with Peking to remain suspended during much of the critical period of deepening U.S. involvement in Laos. When they were resumed in January 1970 at President Richard

M. Nixon's initiative, it was already very late for the United States to garner public support for its actions in Laos. Why U.S. policymakers took so long to appreciate the community of interest that existed between Washington and Peking in preventing Hanoi's total victory in Indochina is a mystery. Dulles's legacy apparently lasted long after his departure from the scene.

In southern Laos, except for occasional long-range guerrilla patrols, all the Ho Chi Minh Trail area remained inviolable to ground penetration,[5] and the only military answer to the growing flow of troops and supplies was air attack. Tonnage transported by Group 559 rose from about 100 tons (91 metric tons) a week in 1963 to about 400 tons (363 metric tons) a week in 1965 and to more than 10,000 tons (9,070 metric tons) a week by 1970. An estimated two thousand to three thousand trucks were on the trail at any one time during the 1969–1973 period. The U.S. bombing campaign against the trail from 1965 to 1973 was the most intensive ever mounted by U.S. forces. The rate of sorties over Laos increased after the partial bombing halt over northern North Vietnam on March 31, 1968, and increased again after the complete halt of bombing of North Vietnam seven months later. The number of sorties flown each day climbed from 120 in 1967 to 400 in 1969, on average. The tonnage of bombs dropped on Laos, most of them on the trail, had been 454,998 (412,683 metric tons) through 1968. During Richard M. Nixon's administration, more than that was dropped each year. When the bombing finally halted in 1973, U.S. aircraft had dropped 2,092,900 tons (1,898,260 metric tons) of bombs on Laos, approximately the total tonnage dropped by U.S. air forces during all of World War II in both the European and Pacific theaters.[6] Yet in spite of use on a vast scale of electronic wizardry—air-dropped sensors, signal relay aircraft, and computer processing of targets and weaponry—it is estimated that the bombing succeeded in destroying only from 15 to 20 percent of the cargo that started down the trail.[7]

From 1965 to 1973 the war seesawed back and forth in northern Laos. Although the royal forces had occasional successes, such as Vang Pao's recapture of the Plain of Jars in an unusual monsoon offensive in 1969, these were isolated events against a background of military stalemate. The North Vietnamese command followed an annual plan of campaigning dictated by the seasons. North Vietnamese army units rotated into Laos at the beginning of each dry season. They operated at regimental level like the 174th Regiment of the 316th Division: first beating back the royal forces from outposts reoccupied during the previous rainy season and supplied for the most part by airdrop, then retiring over the border again to their bases in North Vietnam. As attrition began to take its toll of the hardy Hmong guerrillas, U.S. air power was increasingly relied on to enforce the stalemate.

The U.S. military and paramilitary effort in support of the royal government was under the oversight of the U.S. embassy in Vientiane. Although this effort involved air strikes by aircraft based in Thailand and coordination and supply operations by the CIA and its contractors, including Air America, the U.S. ambassador in Laos had the final word on every detail of a round-the-clock orchestration designed to preserve a precarious stalemate and maintain a low visibility. The ambassadors who achieved this were, successively, Unger, who finally got the CIA under control; William H. Sullivan, who had been Harriman's deputy in the U.S. delegation to the 1961–1962 Geneva Conference; and G. McMurtrie Godley.

The U.S. military establishment appreciated, to a much greater extent than its critics allowed, that bombing civilian populations in Laos was counterproductive to the war effort, and it went to great lengths to avoid such bombing. But the North Vietnamese realized this reservation and involved the civilian population in the areas under their control in military operations as a matter of policy. Civilians were mobilized to repair roads, transport war materials, and store military supplies in villages. This policy resulted in a tradeoff for the North Vietnamese: It undoubtedly lost popular support for the Pathet Lao, but it made a not negligible gain on the U.S. home front, where reports of U.S. air strikes against civilian targets fueled opposition to the war.[8]

THE 1972-1973 NEGOTIATIONS

Apart from the more or less continuous rain of fire along the trail, these years were marked by bursts of bitter fighting but little change in territorial control.[9] Souvanna Phouma maintained contact with Souphanouvong in Sam Neua, occasionally using the ICSC and the Soviet and North Vietnamese ambassadors in Vientiane as messengers. Reestablishment of the coalition was his unchanging goal in spite of being labeled *traitor, capitulationist,* and *tool of the U.S. aggressors* by the Pathet Lao radio. Finally, in October 1972 the North Vietnamese, having negotiated the major components of a cease-fire and political settlement in South Vietnam with President Nixon's national security adviser, Henry Kissinger, gave the go-ahead to the NLHS to negotiate a coalition settlement in Laos. Phoumi Vongvichit, representing the NLHS, and Pheng Phongsavan, representing Souvanna Phouma, opened the negotiations in Vientiane on October 17.

The withdrawal of North Vietnamese troops from Laos had figured as a prominent issue in Kissinger's negotiations with North Vietnamese Politburo member Le Duc Tho in Paris. Although Hanoi, in deference to its fiction that no North Vietnamese troops were in Laos, was unwilling to make a public declaration on this key point, Tho gave Kissinger a written understanding to the effect that North Vietnamese troops were considered "foreign" with respect to Article 20 of the Paris Agreement on Vietnam, which called for withdrawal of foreign troops from Laos. On this basis, Souvanna Phouma welcomed the news of the Paris Agreement, interpreting it as a defeat for the North Vietnamese. At last he would be able, he thought, to work out a political settlement with the NLHS that placed nationalist interests ahead of foreign interests.

Hanoi, for its part, stood to gain from an early cease-fire in Laos, the immediate effect of which would be an end to U.S. air support to the royal forces and to U.S. bombing of the Ho Chi Minh Trail. The withdrawal of its troops from Laos, even if it were made part of a negotiated Laos agreement fixed to a firm deadline, would once again prove impossible to verify. Moreover, U.S. ability to enforce implementation of any agreement was coming to be doubted. The U.S. specialists in the Soviet embassy in Vientiane saw clearly that it would be only a matter of time before Congress, spurred on by press revelations about the so-called secret war the United States was waging in Laos, cut off further appropriations to sustain military actions for any purpose whatsoever.

U.S. bombing of the trails had been effective enough to compel Hanoi to commit some sixty thousand troops to southern Laos alone by early 1973. Although most of these were transport and security forces, they could be redirected at any time to support offensive operations of the thirty-five thousand soldiers in the Pathet Lao army. In addition, in northern Laos there were ten thousand North Vietnamese troops, many of them tied down in fighting the Hmong irregulars. On his side, Souvanna Phouma had about forty-one thousand people in the rightist army, fifty-eight hundred people in the neutralist forces, and Vang Pao's eighteen thousand irregulars, who were paid by the CIA. To help preserve the balance of forces, Souvanna Phouma had had to agree to the deployment in Laos of twenty-seven infantry battalions and three artillery battalions of Thai volunteer troops.

The Paris Agreement on Vietnam was signed on January 27, 1973. On February 9, at a dinner at his residence in Vientiane for Kissinger, who was en route to Hanoi, Souvanna Phouma expressed his faith in the United States, while simultaneously revealing his continued mistrust of Hanoi's intentions. Laos was a very small country, he said, with only 3 million of ancient Lan Xang's 17 million people, and represented a danger to nobody. He counted on his guest to make Laos's neighbors know that the Lao people were pacific by tradition and by religion. "If pressure is kept on the North Vietnamese to understand the risk they run from violating the [Paris] Agreement, then perhaps they will respect the Agreement. . . . Therefore we must count on our great friends the Americans to help us survive. We hope, we dream, that this wish will be granted."[10] Kissinger, however, had not come to Vientiane to extend further the U.S. commitment to defend

Laos. His main purpose, as soon became apparent, was to inform the Laotians that U.S. military support was approaching its end and that, unless they soon accepted whatever settlement was being offered by the NLHS in return for a cease-fire, they stood to lose everything.[11]

When Kissinger reached Hanoi the following day, he was bluntly informed by Le Duc Tho that a withdrawal of North Vietnamese troops from Laos would occur not following a cease-fire there, as he had been led to believe, but after a political settlement. Such a settlement was obviously still months away. Informed of the outcome of Kissinger's visit to Hanoi, Souvanna Phouma, with uncharacteristic pessimism, told reporters that the visit had brought "slim results."[12] The unraveling of Souvanna Phouma's strategy for negotiating a settlement that might have offered the non-Communists in Laos a chance of survival may plausibly be traced to the fact that the North Vietnamese, having received intelligence from their embassy in Vientiane of Kissinger's veritable ultimatum to conclude a settlement without delay, decided to confront Kissinger with a fait accompli in Hanoi. They almost certainly calculated that Kissinger would not jeopardize the process of releasing U.S. prisoners of war, which had begun ten days earlier.

THE 1973 VIENTIANE AGREEMENT

From that point until the signature of the Vientiane Agreement on February 21, Souvanna Phouma's concessions to the NLHS, keenly felt by the rightists, followed in rapid succession. The NLHS negotiators, behind Phoumi Vongvichit's benign smile, succeeded in imposing their view, held since 1969, that Souvanna Phouma's neutralists had merged with the rightist faction and that the object of the negotiations was not a return to the 1962 coalition, but the establishment of an entirely new balance of power in which the "patriotic forces" of the NLHS would be an equal partner with the "Vientiane party." Although it was understood that the government itself (whose actual composition was left to a further round of negotiations) would be headed by Souvanna Phouma, the legislative direction of this government would come from a new, appointed National Political Consultative Council (NPCC) to be headed by Souphanouvong, a decision that left the existing elected National Assembly in limbo. Until the formation of the new government, each side would retain administrative functions in the territory controlled by its forces, with the important exceptions of the towns of Vientiane and Luang Prabang, where Pathet Lao soldiers were to arrive to constitute a mixed security force with the rightists. These political concessions, which were out of line with the military balance of forces on the ground, reflected Souvanna Phouma's fatalism at having been let down once again, as in 1960, by the United States.

The cease-fire took effect at noon on February 22. In the period that followed, the NLHS stretched out the negotiation of a protocol to the Vientiane Agreement as long as possible, in accordance with Hanoi's interest in biding its time and keeping its troops inside Laos, pending the advent of the withdrawal deadline of sixty days after the formation of the new government. In fact, Hanoi, whose agents in South Vietnam—the Provisional Revolutionary Government—were no nearer to achieving success by political means than they had been a decade earlier, needed the continued use of the sanctuary afforded by Laos to prepare their dispositions of troops and supplies for another go-for-broke offensive like those of 1968 and 1972. The 1975 offensive was to be the decisive one.

With the signature of the 1973 Vientiane Agreement, the long stalemate in Laos came to an end. Inexorably, the NLHS began the process of "integrating" the rightist faction and rendering the non-Communist majority powerless—a process that was to go on steadily for the better part of three years and to leave it in final control of the country. Militarily, North Vietnam retained what it had conquered in Laos and achieved unimpeded use of the Ho Chi Minh Trail. In retrospect, the haste with which the agreement was concluded is difficult to explain, except to say that it was a matter of high-level policy, for the U.S. embassy in Vientiane was merely following instructions dictated in Washington at this critical juncture.

Kissinger prided himself on his adherence to the principle of linking the behavior of the Communist powers in all the areas in which vital U.S. interests were at stake.[13] Where Laos was concerned, however, linkage did not work because in orchestrating its strategy in Indochina, Hanoi, not Moscow or Peking, had ultimate control. Like Harriman and Sullivan before him in 1962, Kissinger appears to have overestimated the leverage Moscow and Peking exerted over Hanoi. What can only be described as a miscalculation of strategic proportions was indeed cloaked at the time in the imperatives of high-level policy. But if the outcome could have been obtained at a far earlier date at much less cost, we are entitled to ask, with Souvanna Phouma's son, what was the value of the policy?[14]

THE THIRD COALITION

The protocol giving effect to the Vientiane Agreement was not signed until September 14, following one last coup attempt against Souvanna Phouma by rightist officers. The protocol assigned cabinet posts, set the composition of the NPCC, arranged for the demarcation of a new cease-fire line, and provided for assistance in resettling refugees.

The NLHS lost no time in exploiting the concessions made by Souvanna Phouma. It was helped immeasurably by the popularity of its leader, Prince Souphanouvong. Souphanouvong's arrival in Vientiane on April 3, 1974, provoked scenes of wild enthusiasm reminiscent of his electoral success of 1958; to many in the capital he had become something of a folk hero during the decade he lived an ascetic life in the caves of Sam Neua under the rain of U.S. bombs. He and Souvanna Phouma embraced heartily. The government and the NPCC were constituted two days later.

Its positions in both bodies afforded the NLHS redoubled opportunities for proselytizing and subversion. The fact that all ministers had a vice-minister from the opposite side who had a veto over ministerial decisions gave the NLHS the means to render ineffective the administrative machinery controlled by the rightists and centrists, while it set about creating its own replacement. On the pattern of the Communists in Czechoslovakia in the postwar coalition government, the NLHS set about taking over from within. Souvanna Phouma suffered a heart attack in July. Thereafter, by a well-orchestrated series of strike actions and other public manifestations the NLHS ensured the appearance of the mass appeal of the eighteen-point program for the construction of the fatherland and a draft law on "democratic freedoms" promulgated by the NPCC.

The debacle of the rightists was sealed by military pressure brought to bear by the Pathet Lao forces at the crucial moment. Commentaries broadcast over the Pathet Lao radio (in violation of the Vientiane Agreement), alleging maneuvers of rightist ultrareactionaries against the coalition, provided the necessary background for the decisive move. Progress on placing the twenty-seven landmarks called for in the protocol to show the division of control had been lamentably slow; none had yet been placed along Route 7, where Vang Pao's Hmong irregulars held positions fairly close to the Plain of Jars. Pathet Lao troops now placed flags forward of their own positions, and when Vang Pao's troops removed them they charged violation of the cease-fire. While tension built up, the Pathet Lao maintained their refusal to allow the ICSC, whose mandate had been reaffirmed in the Vientiane Agreement, to investigate.

U.S. reconnaissance flights over Laos, which had been monitoring Hanoi's offensive preparations, halted on June 4, 1974, as the withdrawal of the United States from commitment in Indochina accelerated under the impetus of Watergate, and Hanoi's freedom of action accordingly increased. During December, North Vietnam's 968th Division moved from its base in southern Laos across the border into Kontum and Pleiku provinces, freeing another veteran division, the 320th, to move southward into position for the surprise attack on Ban Me Thuot, planned for March 10, 1975. While attention was focused on Hanoi's final offensive of the twenty-one-year war to overthrow the Saigon government, the Pathet Lao forces along Route 7 made their move.

On March 27, two days after the Politburo in Hanoi reached the decision that a "strategic opportunity"[15] was at hand because of the debacle of the South Vietnamese Army in the Central Highlands, the Pathet Lao launched a strong attack against Vang Pao. The attackers rapidly captured the road junction of Sala Phou Khoun and then drove south along Route 13 as far as Muong Kassy. Souvanna Phouma, wishing to avoid bloodshed, ordered Vang Pao to defend himself as best he could but refused to allow air strikes against the Pathet Lao, who pressed their advantage mercilessly, seeking to destroy the brave Hmong who had stood in their way for more than a decade. Some of the Hmong fled south and were gunned down as they attempted to swim across the river to the Thai side, whereas others sought safety on the heights of the Phou Bia massif to the east.

Meanwhile, a campaign of intimidation against rightist members of the government and officers of the armed forces was gathering momentum in Vientiane. Operating under the umbrella of a coalition of twenty-one "organizations standing for peace and national concord," the demonstrators used inflation and popular grievances to mobilize support in the name of carrying out the eighteen-point program. Souvanna Phouma at first tried to ban the demonstrations but later gave in and sided with their aims. The May 1 holiday provided the pretext for the largest demonstration to date, followed on May 8 by a demonstration against the rightist army and police. Armed Pathet Lao soldiers mingled with the crowd. Although Souvanna Phouma ordered the demonstration stopped, he could not enforce his order. Since the police were the object of the demonstrators' ire, an attempt to disperse the crowd would have led to bloodshed. Four rightist ministers, including the defense minister, who had not been allowed to set foot in the Pathet Lao–controlled zone, fled the country, as did Vang Pao and a number of general officers. Souvanna Phouma strove to replace the cabinet ministers with persons more acceptable to the NLHS. The very meaning of the anti-Communist faction in the coalition had been negated. Demonstrators then occupied the compound of the U.S. aid mission, forcing the termination of the aid program; the departure of the U.S. personnel a few days later was stage-managed in as humiliating a way as possible.

Elsewhere in the country takeovers of government offices and demonstrations led to the entry of Pathet Lao troops into Pakse, Savannakhet, Thakhek, and other towns during May—"to secure their defense." People's revolutionary committees surfaced to seize the administration from the remnants of the royal government, which were purged by denunciations and "people's courts." Military personnel who chose not to flee were summoned to meetings to receive instructions on the integration of the armed forces and were then transported to Sam Neua to begin their reeducation. On August 23, the NLHS completed its seizure of local power with the takeover of the Vientiane city administration by a revolutionary committee.

Behind the screen afforded by popular demonstrations and the movement of Pathet Lao troops into the towns, the North Vietnamese Army moved forward to consolidate its hold over Laos, avoiding the populated centers. In the South, where a special liberated zone had been created following the Pathet Lao takeover of Pakse, three North Vietnamese divisions—the 325th of 1953 fame, the 471st, and the 968th, fresh from the victory of North Vietnamese arms in South Vietnam—took up positions along Laos's border with Cambodia, where the seizure of power by the Khmer Rouge a few weeks before represented a serious setback for Hanoi. For the first time, Thailand felt the menace of regular North Vietnamese troops across its long exposed border on the Mekong.

THE COMMUNIST PUTSCH

As 1975 drew to a close, signs multiplied that the revolution in Laos was nearing its climax, although the exact significance of words and actions remained hidden from all but the tiny handful of Communist leaders who were making the decisions. In October, the NPCC established new screening procedures for electoral candidates that effectively eliminated from contesting all persons who had not supported the NLHS. The NPCC also announced that elections to the new National Assembly would be held on April 4, 1976. Then suddenly, in the last week of November, the NPCC was convoked to meet at Sam Neua.

Also during November, local and provincial elections were held throughout the "new zone"—the former Vientiane government's zone—under a system that abolished the traditional system of popular election of village councils. The general population knew nothing about these elections until the militia personnel called at each household the evening before, distributing cards to eligible voters and assigning each a number. The next morning voters gathered at polling booths set up in the local pagoda. On hearing his name called, the voter presented himself, had his name checked against a master list, and received in return a large ballot on the back of which his number was recorded and bearing a set of numbers corresponding to the candidates (unfamiliar to him) whose names, ages, and neighborhoods were posted on a large bulletin board. The voter then took the ballot into the voting booth, where he crossed off some of the candidates.

On November 28, a huge crowd of demonstrators in Vientiane demanded the dissolution of the coalition government and the NPCC as no longer appropriate to the situation. The next day, the king agreed to abdicate and the prime minister to retire. On December 1 and 2, in a final act a secretly convened Congress of People's Representatives met in the gymnasium of the former U.S. school in Vientiane. Motions put by the NLHS leaders on the tribune received unanimous approbation by those present. The establishment of the Lao People's Democratic Republic (LPDR) was proposed and approved. Souphanouvong was proposed as president and approved. Kaysone was proposed as prime minister and approved. The new government consisted exclusively of NLHS appointees. The third coalition had lasted barely eighteen months.

The adaptability for which Souvanna Phouma was well known was put to a severe test by the dramatic events of 1975. Like the infirm elder statesman Edouard Beneš in Prague in February 1948, however, he bowed to the inevitable with as much grace as he could muster. A number of parallels can be seen between the two sequences of events, perhaps not altogether coincidental. Beneš's coalition government had been paralyzed by the actions of its Communist ministers and action committees had occupied government offices, while in the streets Communist organs spread rumors of a reactionary plot to topple the government. In Prague the presence of Valerian Alexandrovitch Zorin on his grain delivery mission implied the threat of Red Army intervention. In Laos, the presence of North Vietnamese divisions was too well known to require any emphasis, and the fact that they took no actual part in the Communist seizure of control does not diminish the importance of their role. Like Beneš, left by the Western democracies to deal as best he could with his Soviet "allies," Souvanna Phouma emerged with the meaningless title of adviser to the new government and, until his death in 1984, gave unswerving proof of loyalty to the new order.

NOTES

1. Marek Thee, *Notes of a Witness: Laos and the Second Indochinese War* (New York: Random House, 1973), p. 136. The North Vietnamese trusted Thee, who was well known to them from his service in Hanoi and Saigon as counselor of the Polish delegation to the ICSC for nine months in 1955 and as Polish ICSC commissioner in Laos in 1956–1957.

2. Ibid., p. 131.

3. Ibid., p. 145.

4. This criticism implied that Hanoi was banking too much on its second-track and not enough on its first-track strategy.

5. In 1965, North Vietnam set up a special unit, Group 565, to secure the trail from ground attack. When the trail became more important to them because of the threatened closing of the supply port of Sihanoukville in Cambodia in 1970, the North Vietnamese uncharacteristically seized control of two southern Laotian pro-

vincial capitals, Attopeu and Saravane, in the area. The only serious
attempt on the ground to impede the use of the trail was a brief
incursion by the South Vietnamese Army into the Tchepone area
in February 1971. At that time also, for wartime morale reasons
Hanoi began to talk more openly about its operations on the Ho
Chi Minh Trail. See, for instance, the series of articles "We Followed
the Convoys to the Front" by Khanh Van, published in the army
newspaper *Quan Doi Nhan Dan* (Hanoi), March 3–9, 12–20, 1971,
and "Our Troops' Life along the Truong Son Route" by Xuan Hoi
in the same publication, November 29–30, and December 1, 1971.

   The first person to publish a detailed account of the Ho Chi
Minh Trail was a South Vietnamese journalist, Phan Nghi. His
book, *Duong Mon Ho Chi Minh: But Ky Chien Tranh* (The Ho Chi
Minh Trail: War diary), apparently self-published in Saigon, appeared in 1967.

   6. Arnold R. Isaacs, *Without Honor: Defeat in Vietnam and
Cambodia* (Baltimore: Johns Hopkins University Press, 1983), p.
161.

   7. Douglas Pike, "Road to Victory: The Ho Chi Minh Trail,"
War in Peace (London) 5, no. 60 (1984):1196–1199.

   8. The U.S. dilemma of civilian casualties in Laos is perhaps
best described in a novel by a disaffected member of the U.S.
embassy staff. Its two principal Asian characters—a corrupt Thai
police sergeant and a young Lao girl brought to ruin by her
involvement with her U.S. lover—are worthy of classical fiction.
(Jerome Doolittle, *The Bombing Officer* (New York: E. P. Dutton,
1982.) The debate over whether the large number of refugees who
sought the safety of the royal government zone in Laos were fleeing
the U.S. bombing or the conditions of life in the Communist zone
was never conclusively settled.

   9. See the maps showing comparative areas of control in
1962 and 1973, *New York Times*, February 25, 1973.

   10. Henry Kissinger, *Years of Upheaval* (Boston: Little, Brown
and Co., 1982), p. 22.

   11. This was the interpretation of senior officers of the royal
army, who dealt with officials of the U.S. embassy on a day-to-
day basis on such vital matters as air support and supplies. See
Maj. Gen. Oudone Sananikone, *The Royal Lao Army and U.S. Army
Advice and Support* (Washington, D.C.: U.S. Army Center of Military
History, 1983), p. 150.

   12. *New York Times*, February 20, 1973.

13. Henry Kissinger, *White House Years* (Boston: Little, Brown and Co., 1979), p. 129.

14. Prince Mangkra Souvannaphouma, *L'Agonie du Laos* (Paris: Plon, 1976), p. 25.

15. Van Tieng Dung, *Our Great Spring Victory* (New York: Monthly Review Press, 1977), p. 120.

6

Lao People's Democratic Republic (1975–Present)

The Communist movement in Laos is organically inseparable from the Communist movement in Vietnam. This is why Laos's present leaders, in speaking of the history of the movement, refer to *the party* that gave it direction. They mean the party founded by Ho Chi Minh in 1930, the Indochinese Communist party (ICP), and, after its formation in 1955, the Lao People's Revolutionary party (LPRP). The two time periods are merely two phases in one continuous revolutionary process.[1]

The continuity represented by the LPRP's historical origin in Ho's party was so well known that the party's emergence into public view in 1975 from the Sam Neua base area where it had been incubated, sheltered, and directed for twenty years by the Vietnamese Communists came as no surprise. Throughout this period, the LPRP had had to camouflage itself behind the patriotic front to avoid offending the strong popular feeling in Laos that Vietnam was a foreign country with imperialist ambitions. It was no accident that the party's first mass appeal was to the ethnic minorities of the mountains who felt this sense of Laotian nationality least of all the peoples of Laos. The necessity for this camouflage was well understood by observers who followed events in Indochina.

STRATEGY OF SEIZING POWER

During their twenty years of struggle for power, Laos's Communist leaders made use of front organizations and the

105

slogan "Peace, neutrality, independence, democracy, unity, prosperity." The principal front organization was the NLHS, which grouped together all elements of Laotian society that opposed the "feudal, reactionary, puppet government" in Vientiane, and alternately fought and negotiated its way to control over an ever larger sector of Laos.

Although the populist facade of the NLHS concealed the decisions on the most minute matters reached in secret council by LPRP leaders (a process that caused endless delays in negotiations between the NLHS and the other Laotian factions and in decisionmaking within the successive coalition governments), the party never lost sight of the Marxist-Leninist distinction between strategy and tactics. Thus, it allowed the NLHS to enter three coalition governments but viewed these as merely tactical expedients. No consideration was ever given to *sharing* power in the real sense of the term. Concessions were made to the non-Communist nationalists in the form of bargaining over cabinet posts, but the LPRP's ultimate goal was total power and whatever served that goal was desirable. Kaysone Phomvihane wrote the following about those years: "And although in the course of the revolution we had to change our tactics depending on the respective stages of the struggle, to utilize its different forms and methods, and to show flexibility, the fundamental principle of our Party was always that of *violent revolution* and an *offensive strategy.*"[2]

LAOS'S COMMUNIST LEADERS

To carry out such a strategy required people dedicated to their cause. The leaders of the LPRP were such people, veterans of the struggle.

Kaysone Phomvihane

The general secretary of the LPRP is Kaysone Phom-vihane. Born in Savannakhet on December 13, 1920, of a Tonkinese member of the Indochinese civil service, Nguyen Tri Loan, and a Lao mother,[3] Kaysone grew up in a Vietnamese milieu and was sent to attend lycée in Hanoi and then the law faculty of the University of Hanoi. During his student days he did some youth work under the direction of the ICP, and in 1942, according to his brief official biography, he "joined in the militant struggle of the Lao people against the French colonialists and the Japanese invaders." Kaysone's movements during this early period have not been satisfactorily documented.

By 1945 Kaysone had come to Ho Chi Minh's attention. Ho trusted him sufficiently to send him on a mission to infiltrate Oun Sananikone's Free Lao partisans who had taken control of Savannakhet following the Japanese coup de force of March 9. Kaysone may have been among the hundreds of armed Vietnamese who took over the vacated French military camp on the outskirts of town, with Japanese encouragement. However, Oun does not mention Kaysone in his memoirs, in which he described the situation that he and his four hundred soldiers found on arriving in Savannakhet from Thailand and an agreement they reached to cooperate with the Vietnamese in opposing the French. Kaysone did take part in the liberation of Savannakhet that August, according to the official biography. The arrival of Souphanouvong and his Viet Minh bodyguard a few weeks later seems to have overshadowed Kaysone's role in the nationalist movement; the latter played no part in the formation of the first independence government in Vientiane.

Although Souphanouvong remained in Thailand after the French reoccupation of Laos, Kaysone evidently returned to Ho's base area in northern Tonkin, and from 1947 to 1949, when he is said to have "led the war of liberation against the French colonialists in northeast Laos," Kaysone secured his grip on the leadership of the revolution in Laos. During this period, Ho implemented the strategy of establishing a base area along the Vietnam-Laos border from which to launch the Communist revolution in Laos, as opposed to relying on the hit-and-run raids from Thailand mounted by Souphanouvong's followers. Kaysone is credited with having set up the first unit—called the Latsavong unit—of what was to become the Lao Issara army on January 20, 1949 (later renamed the People's Liberation Army of Laos).

Kaysone Phomvihane with Pathet Lao soldiers. (Neo Lao Hak Sat—NLHS—photo)

Kaysone is officially said to have become a member of the ICP in 1949, but Lao sources claim he was not only a member much earlier but also a candidate member of the ICP Central Committee. This chronology accords better with the fact that six years later Kaysone was named general secretary of the still secret Lao Communist party.

Kaysone became defense minister in the "first resistance government" formed in August 1950 under Souphanouvong's titular leadership. This was the first independence government in Laos exclusively under the control of the ICP, and Kaysone's power lay in his role as party leader. He has been the only general secretary of the LPRP since its formation on March 23, 1955, and, as some Lao sources maintain, he probably is simultaneously a secret member of the Vietnamese Communist party. From August 1958, when he was defeated in the National Assembly elections as an NLHS candidate from Attopeu, until December 1975, when he became prime minister of the Lao People's Democratic Republic (LPDR), Kaysone made no public appearances in non-Communist countries.

Kaysone's second name, Phomvihane, was invented like the name Ho Chi Minh. It is the Lao transliteration of Pali Brahma-vihara, meaning the four sublime states of mind to be achieved by the Buddhist monk. These states are loving kindness, compassion, sympathetic joy, and equanimity. The implication was that Comrade Kaysone, as he was commonly called, possessed these attributes.

Souphanouvong

The NLHS was under the titular leadership of Souphanouvong, but the prince's behavior in negotiating with the Vientiane leaders showed that his mandate was tightly circumscribed and that he was obliged to obtain prior agreement from the LPRP leadership on all important matters. Decisions on military matters affecting the Pathet Lao forces were sometimes taken without consulting him at all. Although he was married to a Vietnamese woman, Souphanouvong's royal ancestry must have disqualified him in Ho's eyes from assuming the top leadership of the revolutionary forces in Laos. The LPRP leaders also suspected that he might one day be tempted to seek an independent power base from which to counter Hanoi's domination. Whatever the reality of such a temptation, Souphanouvong's stay in China in the early 1950s no doubt lent some credence to the theory.

The personal popularity that Souphanouvong has always enjoyed among the Lao was a potent asset for the NLHS but also a weapon that could be turned against the Vietnamese. It is highly significant that in May 1975, at the critical moment when the LPRP was fomenting the street demonstrations in Vientiane to swing the balance of power decisively against the rightist faction, Souphanouvong was absent in Sam Neua escorting King Savang Vatthana on a royal visit. The possibility that a person of the prince's caliber might be able to turn the tide of popular emotion to personal advantge so as to cheat the LPRP leaders of power at the final moment must have figured prominently in their plans. A highly embarrassing scene would have occurred if Souphanouvong had questioned, even by vague allusions, how the presence of fifty thousand

Vietnamese soldiers on Laotian soil accorded with the slogan "Peace, neutrality, independence, democracy, unity, prosperity."

Lesser Leaders

The other Communist leaders of Laos are not of Kaysone's stature. The second man in the LPRP Politburo, Nouhak Phoumsavanh, is, like Kaysone, an early recruit whose ties with Vietnam brought him to the attention of the Vietnamese Communists. He is also from Savannakhet and had been operating a bus line between middle Laos and Vinh. By 1954 he was foreign minister in the Pathet Lao resistance government and a member of the DRV delegation at Geneva. He was elected to the National Assembly from Sam Neua in 1958 and reappeared in 1961 as leader of the NLHS delegation to the Ban Namone truce talks. He holds the government posts of deputy prime minister and minister of finance, and is married to a Vietnamese woman.

Phoumi Vongvichit, fourth in rank in the seven-man Politburo, is the son of a governor of Vientiane Province and entered the civil service, becoming secretary to the French resident in Xieng Khouang. He was made governor of Sam Neua Province after 1954. He held ministerial posts with Souphanouvong in the first two coalitions and played a key role in negotiating the agreements leading to the third. He led the NLHS delegation to Geneva in 1961. Perhaps because he is more "Laotian" than others in the LPRP's top leadership, he was trusted by Souvanna Phouma probably more than any other with the exception of Souphanouvong. He holds the government posts of deputy prime minister and minister of education, sports, and religious affairs.

The Politburo is rounded out by Khamtay Siphandone (deputy prime minister and minister of national defense), Phoune Sipraseuth (deputy prime minister and minister of foreign affairs), and Sisomphone Lovansay, a member of the Lao T'ai ethnic group and the only representative of Laos's tribal minorities in the top LPRP leadership. In addition to Kaysone, Nouhak, Khamtay, Phoune, and Sisomphone, the nine-person secretariat consists of Saly Vongkhamsao, Sisavat Keobounphanh, Samane Viyaket, and Maychantane Seng-many. The Central Committee, after the Third Congress in 1982, consisted of forty-nine full members and six alternate members, of whom fifteen had been members of the old ICP.

The LPRP is dominated by the Lao Loum; the ethnic breakdown of the Central Committee after the Third Congress was 79 percent Lao Loum, 15 percent Lao Theung, and 6 percent Lao Soung. These percentages represent a decided shift in balance from earlier years when geographic necessity forced the Communist movement to base itself mainly on the support of the minority tribal groups who inhabited the areas "liberated" at that time. After the LPRP took control of the Mekong valley, it began a vigorous recruiting drive among the Lao Loum. Total membership of the LPRP in 1982 was claimed to be thirty-five thousand.

THE EVENTS OF 1975

The parody of democracy consisting of the elections held in November 1975 marked the end of some six hundred years of village autonomy in Laos[4] and the arrival of Leninist "democratic centralism," which was extended from the so-called new zone into the country as a whole. Those elected in this process were LPRP functionaries, and since the party knew best what was good for the people, they were simply the party's servants.[5] This marked a fundamental change in the relationship between the people and the state. In political terms, the November elections were the point at which the LPRP administration, heretofore carefully cloaked in secrecy, emerged into view. Within a few days the top party hierarchy also symbolically appeared at the tribune of the Congress of People's Representatives in Vientiane on December 1 in the person of Kaysone Phomvihane, who since 1958 had been little more than a name for the people of the non-Communist zone.

The resignation of the coalition government and the National Political Consultative Council (NPCC), the abdication of the king, and the proclamation of the people's republic

were for perhaps the majority of Laotians like lifting a veil.
Since 1973, the people in the non-NLHS zone had been living
in an atmosphere of mixed hopefulness and conciliation. The
Pathet Lao had been greeted with suspicion in Vientiane and
Luang Prabang, initially at least. But with the sudden U.S.
withdrawal of support for the rightists and the genuine
weariness with the long war, this suspicion had given way
to a sort of admiration for the NLHS, the people of the
forest. Notwithstanding the concessions that had been made
to gain the cease-fire and the continued presence in Laos of
North Vietnamese troops, many Laotians were prepared to
take the NLHS spokespersons at their word when they evoked
the reestablishment of a national spirit and impressed on the
people the nobility of joining in the reconstruction. In these
years, the Pathet Lao soldiers in their baggy uniforms and
the NLHS leaders at political rallies in Vientiane and Luang
Prabang achieved the height of their popularity. True, the
old National Assembly had been placed in limbo by the terms
of the 1973 negotiated agreements, but the NPCC, sitting in
Luang Prabang where the king's shadow was ever long, had
provided some measure of reassurance that the country's past
traditions were not being abruptly ruptured.

For these reasons the events of November and December,
which appeared to follow a script in which the non-Communist
Laotians had not been consulted, came as such a shock. Even
the French had not dared to tamper with the system of village
elections, and now this system was abolished. There would
be no National Assembly elections in 1976, as promised by
the NPCC in October, and even the NPCC itself was no
more.[6] The Laotians, who had been prepared to see the NLHS
win some of the seats in the National Assembly usually held
by the old families whose power depended on money and
influence, found themselves overnight living in a country
without a parliament and without a constitution, a country
where the only law in the future would be that of the party,
which proclaimed that these institutions were no longer
appropriate.

The abdication of the king was the hardest blow of all.
The king had, throughout the long war, been circumspect in

his political dealings. On the one hand, his feelings about the Pathet Lao and their links with Hanoi were well known among the Lao; on the other, he had given his steadfast support to Souvanna Phouma as the instrument of reconciliation of all the factions of Laos. Until the last, the NLHS continued to give prominence in its statements to its respect for the throne. The third coalition government had received its investiture from the king in April 1974 with all the traditional pomp and ceremony. The monarchical form of state had been expressly endorsed in the eighteen-point program drawn up by the NPCC barely a year prior to the proclamation of the republic.

The abdication deprived the majority of Laos's inhabitants of their country's soul, both spiritual and temporal. The finality of the act was unprecedented. Even the Lao Issara, in the tempestuous days of October 1945, when they voted to depose King Sisavang Vong for opposing them, had not dared to tamper with the institution of the monarchy itself. In fact, not wishing to be guilty of harming national unity, they had asked the old king to ascend the throne once more a few weeks later.

The actions announced in December 1975 lifted the veil from the reality that had been there all along, a reality suspected but not proved up to that point—the reality of the party. Clues to the nature of this reality were evident in the actions themselves. The Congress of People's Representatives was patterned like an assembly with the same name that met secretly in the mountains of northern Vietnam on August 16, 1945, and prepared the way for the announcement of Ho Chi Minh's republic in Hanoi a few weeks later. The abdication of the king, described as voluntary and "for the good of the people," was of the same cloth as the abdication of Emperor Bao Dai in Vietnam thirty years previously. In each case, the abdicated monarch was named an adviser to the new president.

A MASS EXILE

The sharp turn of political events in Laos represented by the resumption of offensive action by the Pathet Lao forces at the end of March 1975 and the street demonstrations of May bore the clear message for many Laotian non-Communists that the days of the coalition government were numbered and that it was only a matter of time before the Communists took over completely. With the flight of the rightist government ministers, the members in the rightist faction who still held important posts in the administration and the armed forces were left without leaders, as the LPRP intended. The result was an exodus of many of Laos's administrative, technical, and commercial elite who were soon joined by thousands of ordinary villagers, farmers, and small merchants as the economic policies imposed by the new order made themselves felt. This exodus eventually included more than three hundred thousand persons.[7]

Among the sorriest of the exiles were the Hmong, who were virtually destroyed as a significant ethnic group as a result of years of warfare, dislocation, and, finally, a determined extermination campaign mounted against them. After the disastrous defeat of their troops in March and April and the flight of their leader, Vang Pao, the Hmong—men, women, and children—split into two groups. One group, after a long and dangerous march through hostile country, fled into Thailand where twenty-five thousand reached safety. But a larger group, some sixty thousand, retreated to the heights of the Phou Bia massif south of the Plain of Jars where they once again set up the villages that had been displaced so many times and fortified them against attack. Their safe bases to the west, Sam Thong and Long Chen, had been overrun by the advancing Vietnamese, whereas the Pathet Lao converged on Vientiane and Luang Prabang.

Aside from occasional harassing attacks by the Pathet Lao, no serious attempt was made to interfere with the Hmong for more than a year after the Communist takeover. Perhaps the new government assumed that the Hmong would starve to death. In 1977, however, the Phou Bia massif was encircled and attacked by Vietnamese troops backed up by Soviet 130-millimeter long-range artillery. Again, the defenses of the Hmong in the mountains held, and the attackers were driven off. Then in August, Vietnamese forces, unable to penetrate the Hmong ground defenses, began to overfly the redoubt, dropping napalm, gas, and poisons known as trichothecene mycotoxins on the Hmong villages. An unknown number of the Hmong died, while others tried to escape to Thailand. In December alone, twenty-five hundred Hmong arrived at the refugee camp at Nong Khai; this group was said to have included eight thousand at the outset, but many turned back and others were captured or shot by the Pathet Lao along the escape route. By the end of 1979, an estimated three thousand Hmong were crossing into Thailand each month, although this rate subsequently dropped. Thirty-five thousand Hmong refugees are estimated to have been resettled in the United States, six thousand in France, and more than two thousand in Canada, Australia, Argentina, and French Guyana.

RESISTANCE MOVEMENTS

Although the LPRP with the assistance of Vietnamese advisers in its ministries and Vietnamese army units stationed in Laos has been able to consolidate its power in Laos, the regime faces an internal security threat that is not negligible. This threat stems partly from anti-Communist elements that never left Laos and partly from exiles who seek to return from abroad and who have, in some instances, succeeded in enlisting foreign powers in this endeavor.

Such resistance was only sporadic before 1980. The former king, Savang Vatthana, was stripped of his title of adviser to the president and placed under arrest in Sam Neua during 1977, when the regime suspected that he might become the focus of an antigovernment resistance movement. There was also an assassination attempt against Kaysone. However, in 1980 resistance groups carried out a number of hit-and-run raids on installations and army personnel, notably the Vietnamese. These activities have forced the regime to maintain a war footing while it pursues its policies of economic development.

Outside pledges of support for resistance movements have come from China, whose support of an Indochinese Resistance Front would accord with its anti-Hanoi policy generally and with its support of the Khmer Rouge resistance to Vietnamese occupation of Cambodia in particular; and from Thailand at various moments since 1975 when relations between the two countries have become particularly tense. (Foreign relations will be discussed more fully in Chapter 7.) Both countries are in a position to furnish material aid to resistance movements if they choose. But the most effective resistance group has been the Lao People's National Liberation Front, announced on September 15, 1980, in Champassak Province, by four anti-Vietnamese movements representing rightists, neutralists, and ethnic minorities; it has reportedly established contact with resistance groups along the Thailand-Cambodia border and in Cambodia itself. The actual strength of these various groups is difficult to judge.

HANOI'S SATELLITE

As we have seen, Vietnamese troops in Laos moved to forward positions on the borders with Cambodia and Thailand following the Communist takeover in Vientiane in December 1975. Hanoi had reason to expect trouble from Cambodia following the consolidation in power of the Khmer Rouge. In Thailand, Hanoi had long supported subversive activities of antigovernment guerrillas in the northeast. During 1975 and 1976, considerable talk circulated among cadres of the LPRP about Laos's historic claims to the northeast.

If the evidence of a Pathet Lao officer who deserted to Thailand in August 1976 is to be believed, Hanoi had a plan for an invasion of the northeast set for January-February 1977. At the end of May 1976, Hanoi moved seven divisions (sixty to seventy thousand troops) into position on the Mekong in Houei Sai, Oudomsai, Luang Prabang, Thakhek, Savannakhet, and Champassak provinces. But the plan, if it existed, was dropped for one reason or another. In 1977, aside from the reduction of the Hmong, Hanoi was concentrating on the increasingly hostile situation evolving in Phnom Penh and preparing for its first invasion of Cambodia (which failed). In December 1978, however, Vietnamese forces again invaded in greater strength and drove the Khmer Rouge leaders from

Phnom Penh in January 1979. This attack was shortly followed by a limited Chinese invasion of northern Vietnam.

NOTES

1. For example: "This is why, from the moment it came into being, first as the Communist Party of Indochina and then as the Lao People's Revolutionary Party, *the Party* was faced with the immediate task of expelling the colonialists, liberating the nation, and winning the independence and freedom of the country to realize the aspirations of all Lao patriots." (Kaysone Phomvihane, *Revolution in Laos* [Moscow: Progress Publishers, 1981], p. 51 [italics added]).

2. Kaysone, *Revolution*, p. 141 (italics in original).

3. Some Lao sources affirmed that Kaysone's real mother was also Vietnamese. According to this version, after her death Kaysone's father remarried, this time to a Lao.

4. The centuries-old system of administration introduced by the T'ai peoples was based on the *muong*, or district; the *tasseng*, or canton; and the *ban*, or village. The heads of these respective units were the *chao muong*, the *nai tasseng*, and the *pho ban*. In 1973, there were 922 cantons and 12,600 villages in Laos.

5. A Laotian observer of the system in the NLHS zone wrote: "Because of the extreme degree of centralization of power in the hands of the members who constitute the Permanent Bureau of the Central Committee of the Party and the Front, one sees that the mission assigned to the provincial and local administration was to execute faithfully the Permanent Bureau's directives. It follows that this administration enjoys no autonomy of action." (Chou Norindr, "Le Néolaohakxat ou le Front Patriotique Lao et la Révolution Laotienne," unpublished doctoral thesis, Université Sorbonne Nouvelle, January 1980, vol. 1, p. 456.)

6. As a substitute for the NPCC, the Congress of People's Representatives established a Supreme People's Assembly, whose forty-five members were appointed. Aside from Souphanouvong, who presides, they include only second-echelon party functionaries. This body was entrusted with writing a constitution but as of 1984 had only gotten as far as appointing a fifteen-member constitutional commission (Radio Vientiane, May 26, 1984)—which gives some idea of the relative priority the party assigned to this task. The Supreme People's Assembly rarely meets more than once

a year and then only to listen to and approve the reports of the prime minister.

7. *Bangkok Post,* November 25, 1980. In 1984, eighty thousand refugees from Laos were living in Thailand. (*New York Times,* September 20, 1984.)

7
Foreign Relations

The Laotian Communists and their mentors in Hanoi see foreign relations under a dual aspect. One of these—the relationship between states—is a familiar type, involving the everyday work of diplomats and embassies, commercial trade, the negotiation of treaties and alliances, and, if necessary, the issuance of threats and ultimatums, and the waging of war. The other—less familiar to most of us—is equally important: the relationship between Communist parties. In states like Vietnam and Laos, the attitude adopted toward the ruling Communist party of a foreign country like the Soviet Union or China not uncommonly shapes the relationship that exists on a state level. The party of the foreign country is judged according to its interpretation of Marxism-Leninism, the fundamental dogma of Communists the world over, and according to the manner in which this dogma is applied to real-world situations. Thus, the relations between the Vietnamese Communists and the Communists of the USSR and China have experienced ups and downs over the years (a situation readily documented from public statements and actions of the Vietnamese leaders). Since the leaders of the LPRP emerged as sole holders of power in Laos, they have begun to establish a similar track record.

In the cases of relations between ruling parties and parties in non-Communist countries, the situation is more complicated. Sometimes a contradiction is apparent in such cases between the state-state aspect of the relation and its party-party aspect. We have seen, for instance, that for a number of years North Vietnam maintained an embassy in

119

Vientiane, which dealt with Souvanna Phouma as prime minister of the Laotian coalition government (even while he sanctioned U.S. bombing of North Vietnamese troops in Laos), and at the same time maintained a clandestine (though widely known) relationship with the LPRP as the central organ of the Laotian revolution. The contradiction is only apparent, however, since for Marxist-Leninists what matters is *the party's accession to power* and the conflict necessary to achieve this. Interstate conflicts, in this perspective, are merely *situations of which advantage can be taken.* Thus, Ho Chi Minh, following the example of Stalin's allying himself opportunistically with Hitler, was prepared to take full advantage of the conflict between the Japanese and the French in Indochina to advance the cause of the Viet Minh; both Japan and France were imperialistic powers and had nothing in common ideologically with the Viet Minh (indeed, they were enemies of the Viet Minh in a fundamental sense), but this did not prevent Ho's accepting arms from the Japanese after the latter declared the independence of Vietnam, while at the same time feeding tidbits of intelligence about the Japanese order of battle to the OSS.

Under the heading of Laos's foreign relations, therefore, this chapter will describe relations that involve both state-state and ruling party–ruling party aspects (Vietnam, the Soviet Union, China), relations that involve state-state and ruling party–nonruling party aspects (Thailand), and one case (United States) in which the state-state relation is the only important aspect (since the LPRP can realistically expect to gain little from its relation with the Communist party of the United States aside from incidental propaganda support). In addition, the chapter will discuss Laos's relations with international organizations.

VIETNAM: THE "SPECIAL RELATIONSHIP"

Since both the LPRP and the Vietnamese Communist party (VCP) are offshoots of the Indochinese Communist party, their relations cannot be described as those of subservient and dominant partners. Such an interpretation would miss the essence of the relationship, which is one of identity, reflected in their use of the term *special* to describe it. The parties share identity of ideology, identity of program, and identity of means. They are branches of one and the same entity.[1]

This fact imposes a particular perspective in considering Laos's relations with Vietnam. Identity does not preclude diversity but implies a unified control, at which the Vietnamese Communists, with their proven mastery of "front" tactics, excel. Thus, Laos's foreign relations differ from those of Vietnam—a fact that has advantages for both Laos and Vietnam. Any LPDR initiative that actually harmed Vietnam, on the other hand, is unthinkable. So anxious were the successors of Ho Chi Minh to give substance to this *special relationship* that they actually introduced the term publicly several years before their seizure of power in Laos in 1975. But several more years passed before the implications of the term could be fully explained to the outside world.

Since its founding in 1930, the ICP debated the question of its relationship to the revolution in each one of the constituent territories of Indochina—Vietnam, Cambodia, and Laos. In this continuing debate, the Laotians were at a disadvantage because the leadership of the party was Vietnamese from the beginning. Although the 1932 program of the ICP called for the overthrow of the dynasties of Annam, Cambodia, and Laos, not until 1936 was a party committee of Laos established to work for the furtherance of the national revolution there. In succeeding years, influenced by the rapidly changing world situation, the party underwent a number of policy changes; for example, the Central Committee plenum of November 6–8, 1939, called for the creation of a democratic federal Indochinese government, clearly an unrealistic goal.

The ICP also underwent the first of a series of changes of form in response to the tactical needs arising from the situation it faced. On November 11, 1945, the Central Committee announced the party's "voluntary dissolution," a decision motivated by the party's need to collaborate with a wide spectrum of other nationalist groups in opposition to the returning French, and an action described by official party histories today as being purely for form, since it continued to act clandestinely. At its Second Congress, from February 11 to 19, 1951, the ICP "decided to split itself into separate parties of each country."[2]

No separate Communist party for Laos existed at the time of this decision, and the leadership of the revolution in Laos was vested in a steering committee of the alliance of the peoples of Vietnam, Cambodia, and Laos, under Vietnamese control. After the establishment of the Lao People's Party on March 23, 1955, the leadership functions of the steering committee, insofar as Laos was concerned, were transferred to the Bureau of Lao Affairs of the Central Committee of the Vietnamese Workers party (VWP, renamed in 1976 the Vietnamese Communist party). The continuity of personnel in this bureau, so far as it is known, is remarkable. Members include General Phu Thien, alias Thao Chan, an adviser to the first resistance government in 1950 who later headed the Vietnamese mission on the Plain of Jars in 1961–1963; Le Van Hien, who became the first North Vietnamese ambassador in Vientiane; Nguyen Chinh Giao, whom Marek Thee met in Hanoi in 1961 as North Vietnam's expert on Laos; General Nguyen Trong Vinh; and Colonel Vo Van Thanh. By this continuity, the Vietnamese maintained their control over the LPRP.

A top-level Vietnamese party and government delegation, led by VWP First Secretary Le Duan and including a number of members of the Bureau of Lao Affairs, visited Sam Neua from November 2 to 6, 1973, and there introduced the phrase *special relationship*. A joint statement issued on this occasion said: "The Vietnamese and Lao peoples take great pride in the special relationship between them." At this stage, Laotian attention was still focused on the formation of the third coalition government and the LPRP had not yet emerged into public view, blurring the significance of a statement issued in the name of a Laotian delegation in which Le Duan's counterpart was still described as "vice chairman of the NLHS Central Committee."

After the Communist accession to power and the emergence of the LPRP, the implications of the special relationship (in Lao, *kane phoua phan yang phisét*) became clearer. The theme was taken up again by Le Duan when Kaysone, now fully identified as general secretary of the LPRP, visited Hanoi in February 1976. Le Duan explicitly associated the relationship with the late Ho Chi Minh and extended it to cover state-state relations. So it was not a new idea, and it meant more than the natural comradeship between allied people fighting against the same enemy.

Finally, in July 1977, another top-level delegation of the VCP led by Le Duan visited Vientiane to consecrate this special relationship by three historic documents—a twenty-five-year treaty of friendship and cooperation, a border delimitation treaty, and a protocol on assistance and loans. The Vietnamese delegation included Prime Minister Pham Van Dong and Interior Minister Pham Hung, who had been one of the advisers at the 1950 national resistance congress.

The treaty of friendship and cooperation was signed by Dong and Kaysone in their capacities as prime ministers. Its main interest centered on Article 2, which could be interpreted as giving legal sanction to Vietnamese troop presence in Laos. In 1983 these troops reportedly numbered fifty thousand soldiers.[3] Although the contents of the border delimitation treaty remained secret, the new line of the border agreed upon by the two sides was reportedly in Hanoi's favor in the vicinity of Tchepone, Huong Lap having apparently been ceded to Vietnam, and in an area southeast of Sam Neua, also occupied for years by the Vietnamese.[4]

A joint declaration issued at the signing of the treaty made it clear that the special relationship referred to at several points stemmed from history, was a force to be reckoned with in the present, and furthermore would continue to serve as the framework within which the revolution in each country would develop.

> The two sides are very elated and proud at the special, pure and loyal relationship closely binding the Vietnamese and Lao peoples, the Communist Party of Vietnam and the Lao People's Revolutionary Party throughout the thirty years of struggle against the common enemies and which has

continued to strengthen and develop in the new stage of the revolution in each country.

The two sides unanimously noted that the Vietnam-Laos solidarity based on Marxism-Leninism and proletarian internationalism and the principle of each party maintaining its independent policy and of respect for each other's independent policy has considerably increased the strength of each nation and ensured the victorious development of the revolution in each country. The progress of the revolution in each country is closely bound to the fruitful development of the special relationship between the two countries. Proceeding from this vivid reality, the two sides affirmed that the Vietnam-Laos special relationship constitutes a precious tradition, an indestructible force and a law of development of the revolution in each country.[5]

The wording can be interpreted to mean that although each party is to maintain its own *policies* for the present—when the revolution in each country is at a different stage of development—the time may come when the stages of development will permit the unique *identity of the party* to be formalized once again, as it was in the Indochinese Communist party. At such a time, Vietnam and Laos may form a union, much like the USSR, consisting of separate republics led by a single party.

In their relations since December 1975, on both party and governmental levels, Laos and Vietnam continued to show the complete identity of purpose and action characteristic of a single seat of decisionmaking. Army units were repositioned as the new situation allowed and as Hanoi's strategy required. Vietnamese military advisers were reorganized; Group 959 had already terminated its mission in 1973,[6] to be replaced by new organizations, whose identity was not revealed publicly. Vietnamese civilian advisers who had helped in the administration of the Pathet Lao zone—including ensuring the security of the party apparatus—took up similar roles at the national level in the ministries in Vientiane; they had been unable to take over these positions at the time of the coalition government because of the accessibility to outside observation of the ministries.

The direction by Vietnam was most evident in Laos's shifts in economic policy, especially the establishment of agricultural cooperatives and the degree of tolerance toward private enterprise, and changes in foreign policy. Foreign observers reported the coincidental sequences of hard-line and soft-line phases of economic policy in South Vietnam and Laos, for example. The similarity was even more evident in Laos's announced position on events in Cambodia. But the attention the Vietnamese devoted to the most minute details of Laos's public life gave Laotians an even clearer measure of the true extent of Hanoi's control over their country.

The number of Vietnamese civilian advisers in Laos has been placed at six thousand, of whom one thousand are attached to the ministries. These advisers come under the Central Office for Lao Affairs, code-named PC-38, head-quartered in Vientiane, which is attached to the Central Western Affairs Commission of the VCP.[7] The activities of these advisers are made easier by the relative secrecy surrounding the private lives of the LPRP leaders. Rarely seen in public, the top party leaders live in heavily guarded seclusion and travel regularly to Hanoi on unannounced trips.

Security is reportedly maintained by some eight hundred Vietnamese secret police under the control of the Ministry of Interior in Hanoi. They identify potential dissidents in the army and administration and keep track of the movements of foreigners. One estimate places the number of LPRP members who have been reeducated for holding anti-Vietnamese views at twenty-five hundred. Even the nomenclature of government institutions in the LPDR has been changed to conform with the Vietnamese: The former Council of Ministers (Khana Rathamontri) became the Council of Government (Khana Rathaban) after the same body (Hoi Dong Chinh Phu) in Vietnam. A large bust of Ho Chi Minh dominated the proceedings of the Third Congress of the LPRP in 1982.

CHINA

The Chinese leaders watched the rapid U.S. withdrawal from Indochina in the years 1973–1975 with incredulity and dismay. Since 1954, the Chinese had hoped to manipulate events so as to forestall a total victory by Hanoi in the three non-Communist countries left by the Geneva agreements. For Peking, friendly relations with independent and sovereign kingdoms of Laos and Cambodia were preferable.

While giving verbal support to the Pathet Lao against the Phoui Sananikone government at the resumption of the civil war in 1959, Peking had been cautious enough not to arm a movement that it saw as being effectively dominated by Hanoi. Peking strongly backed Souvanna Phouma in his efforts to restore the coalition government. By agreement with the latter, Chinese Army engineers constructed roads in northern Laos to link the kingdom with southern China. These roads had little bearing on the war in Laos but had great strategic importance for China's relations with guerrillas operating in Thailand.

In accord with this overview, Peking strongly backed the Khmer Rouge in alliance with Prince Sihanouk, who lived in Peking from 1970 to 1975. Peking saw in the Khmer Rouge and their virulent hatred of the Vietnamese a chance to block Hanoi's ambitions. Unfortunately for Peking and for the Khmer Rouge, the power struggle that erupted in Peking between the radical Gang of Four and the moderate followers of Chou En-lai, who included Deng Xiaoping, coincided with the deterioration of relations between Vietnam and Cambodia. When the radicals in Peking were crushed in October 1976, Hanoi felt free to move on the Cambodian front to install its own people in power—people who had spent the long war years in Hanoi awaiting this moment.

For the LPRP, which had maintained cordial relations with the Khmer Rouge—Souphanouvong even paid a state visit to Phnom Penh in 1977—the conflict between China and Vietnam over Cambodia meant an agonizing dilemma. After striving in vain to bring about negotiations between Cambodia and Vietnam over the increasingly serious clashes along their common border during winter 1977-1978, and thereby putting off a decision to take sides, the LPRP was finally compelled by circumstances to side with Hanoi. In a statement addressed to Le Duan and Dong in July 1978, Kaysone adopted the phrase "international reactionaries" to refer to the Chinese, in accordance with Hanoi's usage. "We once again reaffirm," Kaysone's statement said, "that we always stand by the struggle to defend the independence, sovereignty and territorial integrity [of Vietnam] against threats, pressure, troublemaking, provocation, violation, slander and sabotage committed by the imperialists and the international reactionaries."[8]

As the Laotian position on the Cambodia issue approached that of Hanoi, relations between Vientiane and Peking soured. The Chinese announced the withdrawal of their engineer troops from Laos at the request of the government. Peking maintained its embassy in Vientiane, however, even after the Chinese attack on Vietnam in February 1979, when Laotian media echoed Hanoi's allegations that Chinese troops were threatening Laos's borders. By numerous indications the LPRP leaders wanted to avoid a complete break with China.

The continuing Chinese threat to Laos, however, had become the pretext for an indefinite extension of the stationing of Vietnamese troops in Laos. As Souphanouvong put it at the 1979 nonaligned conference in Havana:

The presence of Vietnamese troops in our country is necessitated by the common task of defending the independence and security of Laos and Vietnam, which are faced with the danger of aggression by the Chinese expansionists and the imperialists. The presence of Vietnamese troops in Laos, which is not a threat to any country and which stems from the friendship and cooperation treaty between the governments of Laos and Vietnam, conforms with the U.N. Charter and the spirit of the non-aligned principles, particularly Paragraph 119 of the Lima Declaration. This question will disappear as soon as the Chinese threat against my country is brought effectively to an end.[9]

The Mekong River in flood at Vientiane. (Photo by Peter Robinson)

CAMBODIA

The LPDR's relations with Cambodia followed a course dictated by the Vietnamese domination over the LPRP. So long as Hanoi's relationship with the Khmer Rouge was, superficially at least, one of working cooperation, Vientiane was able to maintain harmonious relations with them. The joint Laos-Vietnam declaration of 1977, in fact, voiced support for the Cambodian revolution under the Khmer Rouge leadership. But the situation changed soon afterward.

The LPDR was quick to recognize the new Vietnamese-backed regime of Heng Samrin in Cambodia when it was installed in January 1979 by force of Vietnamese arms. One of the saddest aspects of this episode was that some of the invasion troops were Vietnamese units based in southern Laos. Official denials by LPDR spokespeople were not sufficient to mask the truth that the territory of Laos had been used to launch open aggression against a neighboring state. In Indochina, where precedents count a great deal, the Vietnamese use of Laos for this purpose was an event heavy with significance.

THAILAND

For several hundred years a not inconsiderable portion of today's Thailand was an integral part of Laos. Geographically, this portion is the Korat Plateau, or what the Thai call Isan—the northeast. Consisting of a very dry upland inhospitable to irrigated paddy cultivators, the Isan long remained sparsely populated. However, Lao immigration began in Fa Ngum's day and continued steadily thereafter, accelerated by the deportations that followed the Siamese razing of Vieng Chan in 1829. Today northeast Thailand is inhabited mainly by ethnic Lao Loum who speak Lao.

Along with the Lao, a significant Vietnamese minority settled mainly in the towns along the right bank. These expatriates were naturally sympathetic to the design of establishing an independent Vietnam free of French control, and Ho himself spent some time in 1928–1929 proselytizing in Udorn, Sakon Nakhon, and Nakhon Ratchasima. After the failure of the ICP-inspired uprising against the French in Vietnam in 1930, a number of ICP leaders fled to northeastern Thailand. In 1941, in accordance with an ICP directive to establish such associations wherever possible, a Hoi Viet Kieu Cuu Quoc tai Thai Lao (Vietnamese Overseas Association in Thailand and Laos for the Salvation of the Fatherland) was organized in Udorn. This association was subsequently charged with responsibility for organizing support for the Viet Minh in Thakhek and Savannakhet, and, following the French reoccupation of Laos in 1946 it continued its activities across the river in Thailand.

State-to-State Relations

In the aftermath of the military coup in Bangkok in late 1947, however, the Vietnamese Communists found Thailand less hospitable. After the French took steps toward granting independence to Laos, Thailand's principal concern shifted to measures to stem the growing threat posed by the Vietnamese presence in the kingdom. After the death of Marshal Sarit, his strongly anti-Communist policy was continued by the government of Thanom Kittakachorn. During the 1960s Thailand became an active participant in the war in Laos on the side of the royal government. It allowed the United States to use Thai air bases for bombing the Ho Chi Minh Trail, permitted clandestine U.S. operations in Laos like CIA support for the Hmong irregulars based in Thailand, and finally sent "volunteer" troops to fight on the ground. All this resulted in considerable anti-Thai feeling among the Pathet Lao, which during the war was dominated by hill tribespeople. More significantly, the Thai government's wartime actions made it an enemy in the eyes of the Vietnamese Communists, who moved immediately after the LPRP takeover to establish an armed presence along the Mekong, posing a direct threat to Thailand's northeast.

The Thai government of Seni Pramoj, accepting the inevitable—and demonstrating once again the extraordinary adaptability of Thai governments to changing winds of fortune—stated its intention of fostering good neighborly relations with Vientiane and declared its border closed to refugees from Laos, who had been flooding in since April.

All this changed in October 1976, when the short-lived period of civilian government in Bangkok came to an abrupt end and a new military dictatorship under Thanin Kraivichien took power. Relations between Vientiane and Bangkok deteriorated rapidly in a series of border incidents and mutual recriminations. When Laos and Vietnam signed their friendship and cooperation treaty in 1977, the joint declaration singled out Thailand for particular blame, saying that "the Thailand administration has carried out a hostile policy toward Vietnam and Laos: fostering emigrated Lao reactionaries, interfering in Laos' internal affairs and violating Laos' territory, exerting economic pressures upon Laos, carrying out a policy of repression and terror against Vietnamese residents."

Communist Party Relations

Behind these state relations lay an equally important situation involving Communist party relations and Hanoi's strategy toward Thailand. Since 1965, Hanoi and Peking had both supported armed insurgency in Thailand's northeast, using a network of support bases and training camps in Laos. The exact division of responsibilities remained unclear, but intelligence reports showed that the Chinese used the roads they had constructed through northern Laos for this purpose and the North Vietnamese used their multiple infiltration routes across Laos.

This support for insurgents in the northeast involved a rivalry between Hanoi and Peking that was masked at the time. The principal insurgent organization, the Thai Patriotic Front, followed a pro-Peking line, perhaps because of the support it received. However, after the Communist victories in South Vietnam and Laos, and particularly after the Khmer Rouge victory in Cambodia, continued Chinese support for insurgency in Thailand became untenable. Peking had no interest in promoting an extension of Hanoi's hegemony into Thailand. The Chinese, furthermore, were thoroughly committed to the Khmer Rouge, and once the conflict between the latter and the Vietnamese Communists broke into the open in 1978, Peking needed a secure line of communication to Cambodia, which could only lie through Thailand.

The insurgents in Thailand's northeast had not been faring well in the face of a concerted and sustained effort by the Thai military to root them out. The loss of Chinese support was crucial in further reducing their effectiveness. Defections became numerous. Meanwhile, the remnants of the old, pro-Peking Communist party of Thailand (CPT) sought refuge in Laos after the military coup d'état of October 1976. The violence of this coup and the harsh antileftist bans and penalties that followed produced an outflow of younger leftists, especially hundreds of students and socialist intellectuals, workers, and peasants. Many of these were recruited by Laotian and Vietnamese cadres and directed to training camps in Laos.

The Kraivichien government fell in October 1977, and with the advent of Premier Kriangsak Chamanand's term, a new, more conciliatory policy toward Laos began to be implemented. The rate of gunboat incidents on the Mekong, always regarded by the Lao as a barometer of official relations, fell off sharply, and a trade agreement was signed. In January 1979, as Vietnamese forces were sweeping across Cambodia driving the Khmer Rouge from Phnom Penh into refuge on the border with Thailand, Kriangsak arrived in Vientiane to mark the rapprochement between Vientiane and Bangkok.

An important agreement was announced in a joint communiqué on this occasion: Both sides agreed that they would try to prevent the activities of terrorists across their mutual border. The LPRP decided in that month to expel the CPT remnants from their sanctuaries, most notably the one in Sayaboury Province that had been supplied through the Chinese road network. Following the example set by Ho, who had sold the Vietnamese nationalist Phan Boi Chau to the French Sûreté in Shanghai in June 1925, the LPRP was quite willing to sell the CPT remnants in Laos to the Thai authorities in exchange for a promise that anti-Communist resistance forces would no longer be permitted to operate freely across the Mekong. Kaysone returned the visit to Bangkok in April.

In their exchanges, Kaysone and Kriangsak spoke warmly of their peoples as being "brothers in culture." This description is apt and applies particularly to those living in the northeast, who may be said to be identical twins. At political meetings after the 1973 cease-fire, Pathet Lao cadres recited the historical crimes of the Thai and called for a continuation of the Lao national struggle until all the Lao were reunited. The standard line since 1975, when the LPRP was engaged in a recruiting drive among the Lao Loum, has been that any decision to federate with Laos would have to come from the people of the northeast themselves, according to the last foreign correspondent to be expelled from Laos.[10]

Vietnamese support for an externally inspired, but internally waged, liberation movement in Thailand's northeast represented a graver long-run threat to the Bangkok government than an armed invasion of the type Vietnam mounted against Cambodia. The Khmer Rouge had few friends to aid them except China, and although the invasion was condemned in the United Nations—which refused to seat the Vietnamese-installed puppet government—it succeeded militarily. Thailand, on the other hand, had many friends in Southeast Asia, making an open invasion difficult without fear of retaliation. The Vietnamese residents in the northeast, being a minority, could do little to advance the revolution. But the establishment of the LPDR gave Hanoi an advantage in its objective in this part of Indochina: establishing a majority homeland for the Lao Loum of the northeast. In a Lao liberation movement there, the Vietnamese residents would constitute a redoubtable fifth column.

In June 1979, following a new deterioration in relations between Vientiane and Bangkok, the announcement of the formation of a Thai Isan Liberation party—whose objective appeared to be *anschluss* with Laos—came as no surprise. The new party had its headquarters in Paksane, across the river from the closest point in the northeast to Hanoi. The new party's overt leadership included a group of leaders of the Socialist party of Thailand, among them two former members of the Thai parliament, and trade union activists living in Laos since October 1976.[11]

SOVIET UNION

The victory of the Vietnamese Communists in Indochina gave a strategic advantage to the Soviet Union in its goal of encircling China. To what extent the Soviets benefited specifically from the inclusion of Laos in this acquisition of additional Communist territory, over and above the advantages of the air and naval bases in South Vietnam, is unknown. However, a Soviet presence in Laos rapidly manifested itself to the extent that Soviets in the streets of Vientiane were compared by the Laotians to the departed Americans. Before the end of 1975, an estimated five hundred Soviet technicians and advisers were in Laos.

The LPRP maintains closer relations with the Communist party of the Soviet Union than with any other foreign Communist party except the Vietnamese. Each year has seen a veritable merry-go-round of exchange trips in which LPRP leaders visit Moscow and other capitals in Eastern Europe.

UNITED STATES

The United States maintained its embassy in Vientiane following the expulsion of the U.S. aid mission in May 1975 and the Communist takeover in December 1975. Since the U.S. evacuation from Cambodia and South Vietnam, this has been the only permanent U.S. diplomatic mission in Indochina. The small embassy (about a half dozen staffers headed by a chargé d'affaires) has kept open the possibility of a dialogue on a continuing basis. (The LPDR maintains an embassy with an equally small staff in Washington.)

Prospects for enlarging the slender dialogue between the LPDR and the United States hinge on developments on both sides of the Pacific. In Vientiane, the significant factor is the balance of advice within the LPDR Politburo between the hard-liners who view the United States as the world's major imperialist power, which constitutes a serious threat to Communist rule in Indochina, and the soft-liners who feel that their country could benefit from selectively greater interchanges with the United States without jeopardizing the party's rule. The balance of advice is reflected in statements and actions of the LPDR—official propaganda about sinister U.S. schemes to subvert Laos and destroy the militant solidarity between the LPDR and Vietnam, and, conversely, expressions of a desire for improved relations and occasional gestures of good will.

For Washington, decisions about relations with Laos are enmeshed in the legacy—bureaucratic, legal, and emotional— of a long and bitter war, which cost the lives of many U.S. servicepeople and ended in the humiliation of defeat. An issue of particular importance is that of the persons missing in action (MIA). The LPDR has received a number of U.S. delegations to discuss this problem and in February 1985 for the first time allowed U.S. military personnel to excavate the site of a U.S. wartime plane crash. Another hopeful sign for better relations was the birthday wishes President Ronald Reagan sent to Kaysone Phomvihane in December 1984.

Finally, Laos's continued representation at the United Nations (the country has been a member since December 14, 1955) affords the new regime another window on the non-Communist world, as do its memberships of the International Monetary Fund, the World Bank, and the Asian Development Bank.

NOTES

1. Or, as Amphay Doré described it, the serpent (*naga*) with many heads of Hindu mythology. (*Le Partage du Mékong* [Paris: Encre, 1980], p. 178.)

2. Khaosan Pathet Lao (Vientiane), March 23, 1976, "On the Occasion of the 21st Founding Anniversary of the Lao People's Revolutionary Party, A History of the Lao People's Revolutionary Party."

3. *New York Times*, May 17, 1983. The LPDR armed forces were reported in 1980 to total 55,700 persons. (Martin Stuart-Fox, "Factors Influencing Relations Between the Communist Parties of Thailand and Laos," *Asian Survey* 19, no. 4 (April 1979):341).

4. Stuart-Fox, "Factors," p. 229.

5. Vietnam News Agency (Hanoi), July 19, 1977.

6. *Cuoc Khang Chien Chong My Cuu Nuoc 1954–1975: Nhung Su Kien Quan Su* [The Anti-U.S. Resistance War for National Salvation 1954–1975: Military Events] (Hanoi: War Experiences Recapitulation Committee of the High-Level Military Institute, People's Army Publishing House, 1980), p. 55.

7. It is important to note the similarity in the Vietnamese language between the names of the Central Office for Lao Affairs and the name of the former Central Office for South Vietnam. In Vietnamese shorthand, the former is known as *Cuc C,* the latter as *Cuc R.*

Much of our information about the Vietnamese presence in Laos comes from defectors from the LPDR, some of whom, like

Khamsengkeo Sengsthith, a former bureau director in the Ministry of Health, are high ranking.

8. *International Herald Tribune* (Paris), July 24, 1978.

9. Radio Vientiane, September 21, 1979.

10. Stuart-Fox, "Factors," p. 350.

11. For details on the northeast Thailand liberation movement, see articles in the *Nation Review* (Bangkok), September 5 and October 29, 1984; and John McBeth, "'Foreign Legion' Threat," *Far Eastern Economic Review* (Hong Kong), December 6, 1984.

8

The Economy

Laos still ranks as one of the world's poorest nations, with a per capita Gross National Product (GNP) estimated by the LPDR government in 1983 at only $98.[1] The reality of this statistic has been eased by the fact that Laos's economy is 85 percent agricultural, land has been relatively plentiful, every farmer has been his or her own master, and food for the family has been provided from paddy fields and forest. Laos, however, is now undergoing a transformation to a socialist society in which the state will have a much greater say in what the people produce, sell, and keep for their own needs.

COLONIAL LAOS

The economy of Laos has been based on agriculture since very early times. The Lao Loum cultivated paddy in diked permanent fields, and the hill tribes grew upland rice and other crops by the slash-and-burn method. In the latter technique, the field to be planted, or *rai*, is cleared by burning at the very end of the dry season and the crop is then sown among the remaining tree stumps; a field may be cropped in this manner for two or three years and then left to return to forest for the next twenty years. Both methods of cultivation are dependent on the seasons, and a year of poor rainfall can mean crop failure. Rice production increased during the colonial period under the pressure of population increase and reached an annual average of about 550,000 tons (500,000 metric tons) by 1954. Since colonial times, successive governments have attempted to stamp out the practice of *rai* agriculture because of the damage it does to the forest cover and the problem of soil erosion and degradation it entails.

Livestock raising was important all over Laos. Cattle, buffalo, pigs, and poultry were found on most farms. The extensive forests also played an important part in furnishing all kinds of useful products for everyday life. Commercially valuable forest products included benzoin, the sap of styrax tree used in making perfume, and sticklac, a product produced by insects from groves of the *pois d'angola* tree. Some isolated stands of teak near Pak Lay were also exploited commercially. The most valuable unofficial export, however, was the sap of the opium poppy, grown mainly by the Hmong.

In colonial times, a small export trade developed, even though Laos's economy continued to be mainly based on the self-sufficient village—the basic economic unit—and transportation over any distance was difficult. Laos's principal exports in 1954, in terms of value, were coffee, tobacco, cardamom, hides, and vegetables and fruits. Most exports went to Vietnam, Cambodia, and Thailand. The country's major trading partners for imports in 1954 were Thailand (almost 50 percent), France, and the United States. Imports included textiles, food products, and manufactured goods of all kinds.

Mineral deposits of potentially great value were discovered in Laos in the later colonial period, although early hopes of gold panning around Attopeu proved disappointing. Iron ore was discovered on the Plain of Jars but so far has not been exploited because of prohibitive transportation costs. The discovery of tin ore in Khammouane Province, however, led to development of a mine at Phon Tiou in 1923 by the Paris-based firm of Société d'Etude et d'Exploitation Minières de l'Indochine (SEEMI), which continued operating it until the firm was nationalized in 1977.

Laos possessed great hydroelectric potential with its many rivers; so far only a fraction of this potential has been developed. The only significant industrial development in colonial times, apart from the Phon Tiou mine, consisted of a few lumber mills and rice mills.

The French realized that Laos's greatest need for development of its economy was a modern transportation system. A continuing argument went on in the Indochinese administration about the *déblocage du Laos*. As part of this effort, a road was built the entire length of the Mekong valley, linking Pakse in the south with Luang Prabang in the north. Other roads were built across the mountains linking the Mekong River with the coast of the South China Sea. Sam Neua and Phong Saly, however, remained cut off from the rest of Laos. A project to construct a railway from Savannakhet to the coast never materialized.

INDEPENDENT LAOS

With the advent of independence, planning for the economic development of Laos continued in Vientiane. Such plans remained largely unfulfilled, however, and the single biggest change in the economy in the 1954–1975 period, certainly unforeseen by the economic planners, was the emergence of a consumer-oriented society in the main towns. In view of the strategic importance Laos had assumed in U.S. thinking, the U.S. economic aid mission inaugurated a Commodity Import Program (CIP) designed to soak up paper money and prevent runaway inflation. At this time, the aid program was paying the salaries of the army and providing budget support to the government. Under the CIP, the Ministry of Finance issued licenses to private merchants to import goods, which were paid for in dollars and sold for the Laotian currency, the kip. A Foreign Exchange Operations Fund, with contributions from the United States, Britain, France, Australia, and Japan, maintained the stability of the exchange rate of the kip.

Although some light industry was established in this period, such as a cigarette factory at Vientiane, investment in infrastructure was minimal. In the countryside, the potential development was severely limited by the state of insecurity. U.S. private voluntary agencies accounted for what little development went on in the villages and carried on small-scale but effective efforts to improve agriculture, health, and education. As the war continued, however, many of these dedicated volunteers, frustrated at seeing their efforts repeatedly destroyed by military sweeps, bombing, and evacuation, gave up in disgust; some became vocal critics of the U.S. war effort. A small number, like Edgar "Pop" Buell, a wizened Indiana farmer who went to work for International Voluntary Service (IVS) on the Plain of Jars, remained with the Hmong, acting as a vital liaison with the Americans in Vientiane, until the bitter end. A voluntary organization, the Philippines' Operation Brotherhood (OB), deserves mention for its work, which included operating a hospital in Vientiane.

The exception to the general lack of development work was the Nam Ngum dam, part of the international effort to develop the Mekong valley for the benefit of its riparian countries. This project was started during the war and continued by tacit agreement with only sporadic interference.

The greatest external change affecting Laos in this period was Thailand's development of its road and rail network in the northeast in the late 1950s. As a result of the network, several points in Laos, such as Vientiane and Pakse, were connected cheaply and rapidly with Bangkok and the Gulf of Thailand. At the same time, because of the war Laos's routes to Vietnam and the sea were unusable by those living in the Mekong valley.

In this period, despite Pathet Lao claims of economic development in the liberated zone, changes in the eastern half of the country were due mainly to the exigencies of the war situation. After 1961, Souvanna Phouma's government in Khang Khay issued its own currency, which continued to be used in the liberated zone by the NLHS. Printed in Eastern Europe, the Souvanna kips were regularly exchanged at par value in the area under the Vientiane government's control for arriving refugees.

COMMUNIST LAOS

The new government of the LPDR faced an extremely difficult situation when it took over management of the country's economy in 1975. In the "old liberated areas," as the government referred to the provinces that had come under Pathet Lao control during the war, agriculture and every other kind of productive activity had long since been dislocated by the war. Requisitioning of labor by the Pathet Lao and North Vietnamese—an established practice barely disguised by its "voluntary" label—plus requisitioning of food, billeting of North Vietnamese troops, military operations involving sweeps by troops and artillery exchanges, bombing of military targets by U.S. aircraft using such weapons as antipersonnel bombs and delayed-action fuses, and refugee movements on a large scale all contributed to the economic hardships imposed by the war. Even in areas where people remained to plant crops, they had lost their draft animals and could not do so. In the "new liberated areas," consisting mainly of the Mekong valley towns that were liberated after the 1973 cease-fire, the government faced the prospect of a sudden collapse of a consumer society deprived of its main source of support, U.S. aid. For the people there, the very real problem of inflation dictated a rapid return to self-reliance in basic necessities; thus the government ordered city dwellers to farm neighborhood vegetable plots and ministries and government departments to set up their own farms.

Even keeping the machinery of government functioning presented a major problem because of the disappearance of trained personnel. Of one hundred and twenty thousand civil servants who had served the royal government, forty-eight thousand had fled the country, thirty thousand had been sent to prison, and forty thousand had been sent to reeducation camps by the beginning of 1976. To run the government, the LPDR leaders had the ten thousand cadres who had administered the old liberated areas, plus the Vietnamese cadres who functioned behind the scenes.

The government announced that it planned to build a national and independent economy progressing toward socialism. Its program contained three main guidelines: (1) reduction of the service sector to the benefit of the state sector, implying the nationalization of assets of merchants and lesser measures to control petty traders; (2) development of the state sector, including banking, internal trade, import-export trade, transportation, and formation of cooperatives for agriculture and livestock raising; (3) emphasis on the development of agriculture, mainly by prohibiting *rai* cultivation, development of irrigated rice production, intensification of multiple cropping, and rationalization of labor use by forming mutual aid teams on a village basis. In industrial policy, the government's aims were (1) to restore and maintain existing artisanal and industrial production; (2) to construct agroindustries; and (3) to develop the mining and hydroelectric power sectors. Finally, in terms of external orientation, the government planned to reduce the country's dependence on goods transported through Thailand and increase the use of routes through Vietnam.

Implementation of the government's plans to establish a socialist economy did not proceed as smoothly as it had predicted. Initially, thanks to good rains from June through September, the rice harvest of 1975 proved plentiful. To control hoarding and rises of rice prices, the government banned the sale of rice to private merchants, made compulsory the sale of surplus production to the state at a fixed price, and banned the movement of rice between provinces, although allowing free movement within villages. The government, however, was unable to live up to its commitments to purchase surplus production, and peasants began refusing to accept government vouchers. This peasant resistance, coupled with failure of the rains during 1976, resulted in widespread shortages of rice. Also the ban on *rai* cultivation harmed in particular the livelihood of the hill tribespeople who had traditionally sold part of their harvest as a cash crop; instances were reported of hill villages being forced at gunpoint to relocate in valley bottoms. Finally, reflecting a hard line on economic transformation of the country adopted at an important LPRP conference in December 1976, an unprecedented agricultural tax was imposed retroactively on producers; this decision coincided with the Fourth Congress of the Vietnamese Communist party, which decided on a similarly hard line for southern Vietnam. The agricultural tax was one more weapon in the hands of LPRP cadres in the villages whose insensitivity to the peasantry and their traditional methods of production was becoming notorious.

In June a conversion had been implemented to standardize the country's currency. The kips of the new liberated areas were redeemed for the kips that had been used for years in the old liberated areas at the rate of twenty of the former for one of the latter, or "liberation" kip. The exchange of currency at this depreciated rate meant a gain of purchasing power for the inhabitants of the old liberated areas at the expense of those in the new liberated areas. A further currency change was made in December 1979 when the liberation kip was redeemed in favor of National Bank kip at the rate of 200 for one.

Another poor rice harvest occurred in 1977, again blamed on the weather. Government measures to bring inflation under control, however, appeared to be meeting with success. Free market prices, which had risen by 140 percent in the second half of 1976, rose by only 65 percent during 1977. Between November 1977 and April 1978, prices in the Vientiane market rose by only 15 percent.

In spite of its decision to retreat on attempts to control the market by issuing bans and decrees, the government, in conformity with the December 1976 resolutions, pressed on with its program to form agricultural cooperatives. The first stage envisioned involved forming solidarity groups in the villages, based on mutual labor exchanges that were a feature of the traditional system. The second introduced specialization of labor for each group. The third involved collective labor and payments but with peasants retaining private ownership of land, tools, and draft animals. The fourth stage made the transition to collective ownership of all assets.

In spring 1978, the government accelerated the country-wide campaign to form agricultural cooperatives, which had already been started in areas like the Plain of Jars where the destruction of the old village structures during the war and the resettlement of refugees afterward had made the task relatively easier. The formation of agricultural cooperatives, corresponding to the third stage of the agricultural transformation, was written into the interim three-year development plan covering 1978–1980. The plan's aim was to increase food production, promote exports, expand state trade networks, and raise the number and quality of cadres so as to advance the state to a collective and socialist economy. Again the campaign coincided with the decision taken in Hanoi to develop agricultural collectives in southern Vietnam.

Despite peasant resistance, the number of agricultural cooperatives in the country reached twenty-five hundred by mid-1979, when the government announced that it was halting the creation of new cooperatives and was concentrating on consolidating existing ones—the first step in a drastic change of direction in economic policy. Following a meeting of the LPRP Central Committee, a number of reforms were announced that backed away from the previously set schedule for collectivization. Although socialism remained the ultimate goal, increased production (and therefore incentives) and upgrading living standards were recognized as urgent needs.

Two of the first reform measures were the removal of restrictions on interprovincial trade in November 1979 and on petty trading activities by individual producers in January 1980. Private traders were allowed to import goods freely, on payment of license fees and import duty. A new policy of basing official prices of consumer goods on supply and demand was announced. At the same time, producer prices for rice were raised. Government salaries were also raised, and distribution of goods to officials at low, subsidized prices was halted.

A spontaneous reemergence of private trade and enterprise in the towns and a greater availability of agricultural products resulted from implementation of the economic reforms. Rice production resumed its upward trend and in 1981 reached a record 1,272,000 tons (1,154,000 metric tons), making the LPDR self-sufficient for the first time. More goods were displayed in Laotian markets in 1980 than at any time since 1975. The degree of pragmatism shown by Laos's economic planners throughout—apart from the spasmodic return to doctrinaire Marxist-Leninist treatment of peasants and traders that invariably coincided with important party meetings in Hanoi and Vientiane—facilitated the government's relations with international organizations such as the International Monetary Fund (IMF) and the U.N. Development Program (UNDP), which were largely supportive of Laos's efforts to bring a measure of stability to its economy. In 1981, the government felt confident enough to embark on its first five-year plan.

At present, Laos's land and water resources far exceed their utilization. Only about 1,976,800 acres (800,000 hectares) of land, or 3 percent of the country's total area, are cultivated annually, and these are mostly used for single-cropped rainfed rice production. It has been estimated that approximately 1,482,600 acres (600,000 hectares) of arable land could eventually be brought under irrigation (at an estimated cost of $2.5 billion in 1982 prices). Laos's hydroelectric power generation potential is staggering. It has been calculated that the Mekong River and its tributaries in the LPDR could, in time, generate 18,000 megawatts of electricity from a variety of sites.[2] This figure can be compared with actual electricity generation of 113 megawatts, almost all from the Nam Ngum dam, 90 percent of which is sold to Thailand to earn precious foreign exchange. Thailand's total electricity consumption in 1981 was approximately 2,000 megawatts.

The LPDR has received a steadily increasing amount of foreign aid, principally from the Soviet Union and East European countries, Vietnam, China (until this was halted in 1979), a variety of nonaligned states, various Western countries (except the United States), and international organizations. Foreign aid, now as in the past, is important to Laos's economy and accounts for approximately 80 percent of government revenues. It makes up the imbalance between exports worth $26 million (f.o.b., 1979) and imports worth $88 million (c.i.f., 1979). After the closing of the Foreign Exchange Operations Fund, the Soviet Union stepped in with a 32 million ruble loan to support the value of the kip. In a parallel move, Vietnam made available 17 million dong to finance imports of food, medicine, consumer goods, and other necessities. IMF financial support and guidance have been instrumental in encouraging other donors to support Laos's economy.

The LPDR has received a variety of forms of project aid. For example, the Soviet Union has provided aid for the following projects: the construction of a new town and airport at Phong Savane on the Plain of Jars; the operation of the Phon Tiou tin mine; a high-voltage power line; brick and cement works; and road and bridge construction. Hungary has given aid for irrigation and bridge construction; East Germany, for bicycle-repair and shoe-repair shops; Czechoslovakia, for bridges, forestry, sapphire mining, and vocational training; Vietnam, for forestry, irrigation, and geological prospecting and mining; Sweden, for equipment for forestry and irrigation work; Japan, for road construction; and the Asian Development Bank, for hydroelectric power development. The World Bank's International Development Association has given five credits, totaling $53.2 million, for agriculture and rural development. In addition, the Soviet Union and other countries have financed numerous scholarships for Laotians to study abroad.

NOTES

1. Submission made to the Round Table on the Least Developed Countries of Asia and the Pacific, Geneva, May 1983. The sectoral breakdown of contributions to GNP was agriculture and forestry, 85 percent; industry, 6 percent; trade, 4 percent; and construction, 3 percent.
2. Interim Mekong Committee, various reports.

9

Culture and Society

The culture and society of Laos are recognized as distinct in Southeast Asia, although they have strong roots in many nearby countries. Laos has its own spoken and written language, and unique music, architecture, handicrafts, manners of dress, and popular customs. The present government, stemming as it does from a nationalist movement, has accentuated these particularities insofar as they do not conflict with the revolutionary ideal of "socialist man," for instance, legislating the use of the Lao language in place of French and encouraging the wearing of Laotian dress.

PHILOSOPHY AND RELIGION

Theravada Buddhism

The early inhabitants of Laos were animists, and still today the invocation and propitiation of spirits (*phi*), which lurk near every village, remain concerns for a large segment of the population, especially among the hill tribes. By the time of Fa Ngum's reign, however, Theravada Buddhism had spread into Laos and taken root as the religion of the Lao Loum and the Lao T'ai. The followers of Theravada Buddhism have not adopted a militant posture toward nonbelievers, and consequently a large degree of coexistence can be found between animism and Theravada Buddhism in Laos.

Theravada Buddhism is ideally suited to this kind of coexistence. This form of Buddhism counsels the believer to hold a profound reverence for the historic Buddha, his teach-

147

ings (Dhamma), and the order he founded (Sangha), called
the three jewels (Triratna) of Buddhism. Each individual is
called upon to work out his or her own salvation by faithful
adherence to the way demonstrated by the Buddha. Ideally,
this way is along the eightfold path, whose prescription is
characterized by tolerance and enlightenment. Thus, Theravada Buddhism has a natural tendency to assimilate other
myths and rituals, leading to periodic attempts on the part
of reformers to purify Buddhist practices.

The Buddhist Sangha, or order of monks, has traditionally
played an important role in the society of Laos, ensuring not
only its spiritual cohesion but also its economic stability and
well-being. The pagoda (wat) is the center of village life, and
the Buddhist followers acquire merit (punna) in the next life
by maintaining the pagoda and feeding its monks. Before the
arrival of the French and the establishment of state schools,
the pagodas provided the only schooling for children. Many
Buddhist monks were also healers.

At the age of twenty-one, any Laotian man becomes
qualified to enter the Sangha. For twenty-four hours before
his ordination, which occurs on the fifteenth day of the sixth
month, the young man meditates for a period to show his
gratitude toward his parents as well as his piety. After spending
a minimum of seven days in the pagoda, the young man
earns the title of Thit (Venerable). Many young men leave
the Sangha at this time, but others remain for longer periods,
or even for life.

The three basic requirements for membership in the
Sangha are poverty, celibacy, and inoffensiveness. At their
ordination, monks take vows to observe the commandments,
which forbid them to destroy life of any kind, steal, commit
adultery, tell a falsehood, use intoxicating drink, eat at for-
bidden times, attend worldly amusements, use perfume or
ornaments, sleep on high beds, or accept money. Each morning
the faithful kneel down and offer food to a passing line of
monks tending their begging bowls; the monks are not allowed
by their oath of poverty to work for a living. Monks are
identified with the Buddha himself. They are considered
infallible and are the object of popular veneration for as long

as they wear the saffron robe. Even the king bowed to the monks.

Buddhism constituted a powerful buttress for the established social and political order. The New Year ceremonies (Pi may), held every April and May in Luang Prabang, centered on the sacred image of Buddha, the Prabang, which was both the palladium of the dynasty that had ruled Laos since Fa Ngum's day and a symbol of the authority and standing of the Sangha. In these ceremonies, the king, who was the protector of the religion as well as the embodiment of the nation's sovereignty, recognized the higher spiritual power and thereby reinforced his own temporal power by becoming the means for transferring higher truth from the spiritual to the mundane realm for the benefit of the people. At one level the king derived his right to rule from his royal lineage, but a higher legitimation was provided by his relationship to a higher truth.[1]

The LPRP and Buddhism

Since respect for the Buddhist religion and for the throne had figured so prominently in NLHS statements, the abrupt abdication of the king and resulting popular feeling confronted the LPRP leaders with a major religious and political problem. Moreover, the subsequent arrest of Savang Vatthana, his wife, and son; his forced removal from the private house in Luang Prabang where he lived following his abdication; and the unannounced disappearance of the Prabang from its pagoda were additional shocks for the average Laotian. The LPRP, realizing this, refrained from attempting an all-out campaign against the Sangha and instead engaged in a subtle, drawn-out effort to change the institutions of Theravada Buddhism gradually to accord with its political imperatives. And where concessions were judged to be necessary, the regime made them.

When the LPDR was established, about eight hundred pagodas and fifteen thousand monks and novices lived in Laos. The Sangha, with its deep roots in Lao society (reinforced by the fact that nearly every male had at some time been a

Village near Vientiane. (Photo by Peter Robinson)

member), could not be expected to transfer its legitimation
of political authority overnight to the LPRP regime. After all,
all important decisions of the LPRP regime were made by
the seven men who sat in the Politburo, then endorsed by
the forty-nine-member Central Committee, and finally enforced by the thirty-five thousand party members. The LPRP
saw itself as entrusted with the historic mission of establishing
the dictatorship exercised by the party on behalf of the
worker-peasant alliance of all ethnic groups, in accordance
with the tenets of Marxism-Leninism. It had not even gone
through the formality of holding a plebiscite on its seizure
of power; the ratification of the decision to abolish the
monarchy and the provisional government of national union

and to establish a people's democratic republic were obtained from a congress of party functionaries called people's representatives.

For this reason, the LPRP had to effect a transition to new forms and institutions that had no basis in the experience of Laotian people. And in this transition, the Sangha was called upon to play an important role. The king, therefore, was not executed but instead was named supreme adviser to the president of the People's Democratic Republic (just as Emperor Bao Dai, in 1945, had been appointed immediately after his abdication to the meaningless post of adviser to Ho's republic), and the crown prince was made a member of the Supreme People's Assembly. These proved short-term appointments, designed to cushion the initial shock to public opinion. The Sangha itself was preserved but was subjected to new regulations and restrictions, and its body of Buddhist scripture was rewritten by a committee of monks convened by the LPRP to modernize both canonical and extracanonical texts.

In the interest of this transition, the LPRP stepped up its long-time propagandizing effort among Buddhist monks, begun in the old liberated area and now extended to the new liberated area. This campaign was intended to minimize the seemingly irreconcilable contradictions between Buddhism and Marxism-Leninism: Buddhism has a spiritual vision of the universe and condemns all worldly utopias whereas Marxism-Leninism denies all religions and bases its hopes for the future on the material world; Buddhism preaches harmony while Marxism-Leninism preaches the inevitability of class struggle and violence.

To minimize these contradictions, the LPRP tried to portray the future Buddha as an early, prescientific revolutionary who, by leaving his palace and renouncing succession to his father's throne, called into question the value of wealth and social standing. The LPRP pointed out that the future Buddha founded a community in which everyone was treated equally and in which a minimum of material well-being was considered essential for the individual's practice of virtue.[2]

The transition was facilitated by enveloping the Sangha in various regulations, some of which provoked popular resistance and were later amended or withdrawn. Monks were prevailed upon to attend political reeducation seminars where they were encouraged to adopt progressive attitudes and to prove themselves by communicating the LPRP's policies to the mass of the people. The ceremonial fans of senior monks were symbolically broken, and under close LPRP supervision the Sangha (previously divided into two major sects) was restructured as a single Union of Lao Buddhists, with officeholders appointed only with party approval. These now participated in religious ceremonies such as the That Luang festival and attended state functions and even international conferences.[3]

Spirit cults, of course, had been proscribed at an early date by the LPRP; this ban affected mainly the hill tribespeople. When the LPRP forbade people to engage in the begging ritual of the monks every morning on the ground that monks, like other citizens, should work for their living, the prohibition was deeply resented by the Lao. Consequently, the prohibition was relaxed to allow rice to be given to the monks, but not vegetables, which the monks had to cultivate in their own gardens. The party then attempted to regulate the giving of rice (at a time when rice was scarce) by designating the amounts and offerers in each neighborhood. This regulation was withdrawn, however, when popular feeling that giving rice in this way no longer amounted to a meritorious act grew to the point of inciting evasion.

On the whole, then, the regime has had to proceed slowly in its efforts to transform the institutions of Theravada Buddhism. True, the pagodas have not been razed, as they were in Cambodia by the Khmer Rouge, and Laos remains today a rare example of the coexistence of Theravada Buddhism and Marxism-Leninism. The current attitude of the LPRP appears to be that the Sangha is permitted to continue its functions of ministering to the needs of the individual (and, in cases where such ministrations are socially useful, as where monks act as public health workers, the Sangha is actually encouraged) but must not compete with the party in political and economic affairs.

Few Laotians doubt that the LPRP would move much further toward limiting this potential rival authority if it could get away with it. They point to the most ominous trial balloon to date: an attempt by zealous party cadres at Muong Nane near Luang Prabang in 1978 to proscribe the practice of Buddhism by forbidding young men to don the saffron robe, by banning the giving of rice to the monks, and by prohibiting attendance at the pagodas on the ground that Buddhism was pure superstition and contrary to Marxism-Leninism. The order was quietly withdrawn after complaints were lodged with the union of Lao Buddhists.

How has the individual's place in society been changed by the new regime's avowed intention of moving toward the new "socialist man"? Under the old order, the individual was not uncommonly victimized by the arbitrary or corrupt exercise of power by local officials, and access to the elite at the top was strictly limited by education and wealth. The individual could seek redress, however, through a network of connections consisting of family members or village monks. The individual's freedom inside his own village, moreover, was preserved by the tradition that village affairs were exclusively the responsibility of the elected village council and its headperson.

The new order fundamentally altered this village administration, and the changes were shocking to many who had not previously experienced life in the old liberated area. The state had at last forced the gates of the village: The word of neither the headperson nor the elected council carried any further weight. In the absence of any constitution, or even law, matters were decided not by the administration but by the parallel hierarchy—the party—whose cadres, enlightened by the farsighted leadership of the party, applied their revolutionary justice without the possibility of appeal.

CREATIVE AND PRACTICAL ARTS

Music

Music forms an important part of Laotian life. Villagers awake to the deep sound of the gong being struck at the pagoda. Laotian music is composed mainly for the *khen*, a hand-held pipe organ that is the national musical instrument. Laotian music also includes pieces for an orchestra composed of flutes, clarinets, solo or grouped gongs, xylophones with bamboo crosspieces, drums, cymbals, and two-string violins. The scale of Laotian music is pentatonic, and the orchestral music is polyphonic. Often music accompanies singing and dancing. Marionettes and actors' theater are also very popular, and performances are usually in the open during the dry season, accompanied by choirs, recitals, and dances.

Literature

Laotian literature, like that of Cambodia and Thailand, bears the marked imprint of Indian influence in its forms and themes. Unfortunately, many of the once extensive collections of manuscripts were taken away to Bangkok following the razing of Vieng Chan in 1829. The Tripitaka (Three Baskets) texts, written in Pali, are basic to the literary tradition of Laos. Some, like the Paritta texts, are more widely known because of their practical usage; these consist of rhythmic verse, a kind of litany, recommended by Buddha as a protection against harm.

The religious literature deals with stories of Buddha, saints, and places where Buddhism is practiced. The most popular accounts are taken from the Indian jatakas, stories about Buddha's birth and previous forms of existence. Prain (Indra) is a particularly popular figure in Laotian religious literature.

Laotian popular stories and novels are traditional, many of them based on the Indian Panchatantra. The preferred form is a long verse story dealing with adventure and the supernatural. Personification of animals is a predominant motif in Laotian novels. Many stories and poems have been transmitted orally by balladeers. Epic poems, such as the seventeenth-century poem *Sin Xay* by Thao Pangkham, were sung or chanted to musical accompaniment. The singing tradition, represented by the *mohlam*, continued until modern times.

The chronicles of Laos's history were written in Pali by unknown authors. The most famous of these is the *Nilan*

Khun Borom (*History of King Borom*). There were various sets of annals such as the *Ponsavadan Muan Lao* (*The Annals of Laos*) and the *Ponsavadan Kasat Vieng Chan* (*The Annals of the Kings of Vieng Chan*), the latter having been destroyed.

A fresh burst of creativity in Laotian literature occurred with the nationalist resurgence of the 1940s. Some authors, like Katay Don Sasorith, who was intimately involved in political movements, wrote in French, whereas others, like the Pali teacher Maha Sila Viravong, Thao Kene, Phouvong Phimmasone, and Somchine Pierre Nginn, wrote in their native language. By 1953, the Lao Literary Committee had begun publication of *Wannakhadisan,* a magazine devoted to articles on Lao language and culture.

Among important memoirs of nationalist leaders were those by Prince Phetsarath, published in Thai in 1956 under the pseudonym "3349," and by Oun Sananikone, published in serial form in the Vientiane newspaper *Siang Seri* in the late 1960s.

Journalism

Political journalism is represented by Sisouk na Champassak's *Tempête sur le Laos,* first published in Paris in 1961 and translated into English. Accounts of recent events by LPRP figures such as Kaysone and Phoumi Vongvichit, whose books have been published in Vientiane and abroad, closely follow the Communist party line.

Laotian newspaper journalism, while never reaching the proliferation evident in Cambodia under Prince Sihanouk or South Vietnam in the years 1954 to 1975, nevertheless showed a surprising degree of development. Some politicians, after the example of Sihanouk, published their own newspapers to express their views or those of their party. Such was the case of *Sieng Laxa Done,* a bimonthly newspaper published at Pakse in a French edition of eight hundred and fifty copies and a Lao edition of one thousand copies by Katay's Progressive party in the 1950s. Also dating from the 1950s were *Lao May,* a weekly edited by Bong Souvannavong (one thousand copies), and *Sieng Lao,* a bimonthly edited by Kou Voravong until his assassination in 1954 (one thousand copies), both in Vientiane.

In a more scholarly vein, the quarterly *Bulletin des Amis du Royaume Lao,* published in Vientiane from 1970 to 1975, was a modest attempt to provide a forum for articles on Laos's history, geography, language, and culture generally, in the tradition of the French-language journals *France-Asie,* once published in Saigon, and the *Bulletin des Amis du Vieux-Hué,* once published in Hué.

At present, publication of journals differing in political viewpoint from the LPRP—the sole source of truth in Laos—is not permitted. The LPRP's official newspaper, *Pasason* (The People), has been published daily in Vientiane since 1975 by the Press Department of the Ministry of Information. It consists of four pages: Page 1 reports party affairs and editorials that carry the party line; page 2 carries provincial news, a regular youth forum, and a regular column titled "The Tradition of Struggle"; page 3 consists of lessons in dialectic materialism and revolutionary poems; and page 4 carries article continuations and a small amount of international news.

EDUCATION

The traditional education system in Laos was the network of pagoda schools run by the Sangha. The teachers were monks appointed by the head of the pagoda or laymen who had once been monks. Classes were held in the courtyard of the pagoda. Instruction was usually oral, since writing materials were scarce, and consisted of memorized lessons, recited verse, and singing. Subjects studied included religious and domestic ethics, the Lao language, *tam* characters for the purpose of reading and transcribing sermons and prayers in Pali or Sanskrit, and some manual skills such as carving, painting, or decorating.

After the establishment of the French protectorate, secular schools were created to train Laotians for the civil service. By 1905 there were two such schools. Thereafter the number grew, the secular schools coexisting with the pagoda schools until the two systems were merged in 1946 under the Ministry of Education. The French language was part of the curriculum from earliest days, and Vietnamese teachers, of whom there were many, mainly used French. The number of primary schools grew from slightly under one hundred in 1940 to about 550 in 1950, and the enrollment grew from about six thousand to thirty-seven thousand pupils in the same period.[4]

As part of the renewed French effort to educate the Laotians after 1946, provincial high schools were founded at Pakse, Luang Prabang, Savannakhet, and Vientiane (the Lycée Pavie). Inadequate knowledge of French, however, prevented the expansion of secondary education in Laos, since few students could pass the French entrance exam.

Although the official language of instruction after independence became Lao, French continued to be widely used, and French teachers came to work in large numbers in Laos. The advantages of an education abroad continued to draw ever increasing numbers of aspiring students to study in France. The U.S. aid program, attempting to reverse the dominance of French, financed construction of four technical schools explicitly for instruction in Lao, funded teacher-training programs, and pressured the royal government to accelerate its primary school building program. Naturally, however, in war conditions little of substance could be done to make mass education available.

When the LPDR was established, a policy of providing a minimum basic education in the shortest time for the maximum number of people was enacted. This policy has yielded good results, reflected in statistics on education released by the government. Part of this success has been due to the personal dedication of Minister of Education Phoumi Vongvichit. The enrollments in primary and secondary schools have risen rapidly, reaching three hundred and fifty thousand in 1979 and six hundred thousand in 1983. Currently, more than 75 percent of children aged five to eleven attend primary school, as opposed to less than 50 percent under the old regime. The percentage of young people between the ages of twelve and twenty-five attending secondary and higher level schools rose from 2 percent in 1974 to 10 percent in 1980.

DOMESTIC LIFE

Relationships between the Sexes

Another aspect of the modernization process attributable to the LPRP is the changing relationship of the sexes. In traditional Laos, the engagement of a young couple was the object of considerable ritual, and the parents of the groom- and bride-to-be made the major decisions for the couple. In a predominantly village society, such a system may not have lent itself to abuse, since young children grew up knowing one another in a rather restricted circle of friends. Nor was it considered offensive that the man's role was primarily to work the family rice fields or hunt in the forest, whereas his wife remained at home to cook and raise small children. On this basis, men and women shared tasks and rewards equally. If anything, Laotian society probably had fewer tales of the tyranny of mothers-in-law over their daughters-in-law than other Asian societies. At present, the LPRP seems to be gradually nudging young people to make their own personal decisions, but has not given special emphasis to women as leaders. Of the forty-nine members and six alternate members of the LPRP Central Committee elected at the Third Congress in 1982, only four were women. But then, women have never figured prominently in the history of Laos, in sharp contrast to Vietnamese history.

Dwellings

Wood has been the traditional building material of Laos. As in Cambodia, even the royal palaces were built of wood and stood on piles, with the number of wings determined by the rank of the occupants. Above the throne room of the palace in Luang Prabang, regarded as the axis of the world, rose seven successive tiers of eaves, corresponding to the seven celestial paradises of Brahmanism.

Dwellings in Laos are constructed mainly of wood and bamboo and stand on piles, in the case of the Lao, or on the ground with bare earth floors, in the case of the Hmong.

Lao girl weaving. (Photo by Peter Robinson)

Most houses have two or three rooms, sometimes partitioned by curtains for privacy. Furnishings are sparse. In traditional Lao houses, no nails were used; pegs and bamboo or rattan ties held the various pieces together. The shape was usually rectangular, with ridged roofs and wide, open verandas suitable for ventilation. Floors were made of wood or flattened bamboo, walls of wooden boards or woven bamboo. Roofs were made of wooden or bamboo shingles, thatch, or nowadays of sheets of galvanized iron. The space beneath the floor of the Lao house was used for storage or keeping animals. Because it remains cool in the hot season, this space was also commonly used for work such as weaving or basket-making.

Dress

In Laos, dress varies according to ethnic group. Thus, ethnic affiliation may be immediately detected by looking at clothing, jewelry, or other personal ornamentation. Even among the lowland Lao, cloth weave and color pattern, or the style of wearing the chignon, are so many clues to the place a person calls home.

The *sinh*, the characteristic Lao skirt, is made from a piece of brocade about a yard wide and two yards long, combined with narrower pieces called the head (*hoa sinh*) and foot (*tin sinh*) that form borders. The *sinh* and a matching shawl, about a foot wide and two and a half yards long, are traditionally woven at home on a hand loom from materials readily at hand—cotton or silk (the raising of silkworms is an integral part of Lao village life).

The *sinh* is wapped around the waist. In earlier times it was simply tucked in, but more recently the practice is to hold it in place by means of a belt formed of metal rings or buckles. The foot and head are often decorated with gold or silver threadwork. The shawl, worn over the left shoulder and under the right arm, is usually of a lighter color than the *sinh*, which originally was dark green or dark red but in modern times has taken on any number of hues.

Women wear a single-color blouse with the *sinh*. In Luang Prabang this is generally long sleeved and may be quite elaborate, with overlapping ends that tuck in at the waist and with an embroidered border around the neck. In the south the blouse has sleeves three-quarter length or shorter. For formal evening wear, the right shoulder is left bare. Sandals serve for footwear.

Ornamentation among Lao women includes necklaces, bracelets, rings, earrings, and a hairpin. This last is stuck through the chignon that women wear (except the elderly, who crop their hair short). The chignon is worn high on the back of the head, to one side Luang Prabang–style, or low on the nape of the neck in Vientiane and the south.

Among several of Laos's many ethnic minorities such ornamentation is also common. It even reaches staggering proportions in the case of Hmong women, who festoon themselves with many silver necklaces, a sign of wealth. A feature of clothing among the minorities is the use made of embroidery on many types of cloth. Headgear includes a variety of turbans.

Lao men have traditionally worn the *sampot,* a knickerlike garment made of brocade, and a scarf. This was the dress of official ceremonies under the monarchy. Western-style trousers and jackets, however, were adopted for everyday wear under the protectorate.

Cuisine

Laotian cuisine is unique. Its main ingredients (with their equivalents in Lao) are rice, either glutinous (*khao nyao*), nonglutinous (*khao chao*), or rice vermicelli (*khao poon*); fish (*pa*), of which the vegetarian catfish (*pa beuk*) is a staple, often eaten with fish sauce (*nam pa*); and meat, often eaten raw chopped or pounded (*lap*). Water buffalo, pork, chicken, and duck are the most commonly eaten meats, and game, such as wild chicken, quail, small birds, deer, water monitors, and snakes, serves as a supplement. The main vegetables used in Lao cuisine are eggplant, spinach, water spinach (or swamp cabbage), shallots, beans, bamboo shoots, and mushrooms. Salad leaves are used for wrapping. Condiments include coconut, tamarind, citronella, ginger, and hot peppers.

The equipment for preparing meals includes a stove, usually fired by wood or charcoal, and a wok, and utensils for serving, soup bowls, trays, and spoons. Sticky rice is used for pushing and sopping up; each eater uses fingers and has an individual basket of this rice. Those eating sit on the ground and eat off a low bamboo table.

In the *baci* ceremony, which marks any important occasion, people sit in a circle around the centerpiece of a tree made from banana leaves and flowers surrounded by symbolic foods. A monk or "magic person" intones appropriate prayers and benedictions. Then the person being honored has food placed in hand and white cotton strips tied around the wrists; these strips must never be cut, and should not be removed for at least three days.

NOTES

1. For a fuller discussion of the legitimation provided by the Sangha and the problems this has posed for Laos's new rulers, see Martin Stuart-Fox, "Marxism and Theravada Buddhism: The Legitimation of Political Authority in Laos," *Pacific Affairs* 56, no. 3 (Fall 1983):428–454.

2. See Pierre-Bernard Lafont, "Buddhism in Contemporary Laos," in Martin Stuart-Fox, ed., *Contemporary Laos: Studies in the Politics and Society of the Lao People's Democratic Republic* (St. Lucia, Australia: University of Queensland Press, 1982), p. 150.

3. Stuart-Fox, "Marxism and Theravada Buddhism," p. 447.

4. Somlith Pathammavong, "Compulsory Education in Laos," in Charles Bilodeau, Somlith Pathammavong, and Le Quang Hong, *Compulsory Education in Cambodia, Laos and Viet-Nam* (Paris: UNESCO, 1955), pp. 71–111.

10

Prospects

What are the prospects for the survival of Laos as a
national entity? In the contest between Theravada Buddhism
and Marxism-Leninism, which will prove stronger? (Laos is
one of only two countries in the world with the traditional
religion of Theravada Buddhism to have adopted Marxism-
Leninism as its governing ideology.) Will the government of
the Lao People's Democratic Republic have more success than
previous governments in integrating the country's numerous
ethnic minorities? Are the leaders of the LPRP inexorably
bound to follow the dictates of Hanoi in internal political,
economic, and foreign affairs, or are they likely to see Laos's
interest in affirming a separate national identity?

The answers to these questions depend to a great extent
on our reading of history. The Lao were basically an inland
people, but throughout their recorded history they had contact
with their neighbors because of the valleys and rivers that
afforded their principal means of communication and trade.
Sometimes these contacts proved disastrous, as when the
country was invaded by the Vietnamese, the Siamese, the
Burmese, or in more modern times the Chinese. Although
these invasions were not always without the pretext of lending
support to a pretender to the throne, Laos's rulers appear to
have attempted to maintain a balance between their more
fearsome neighbors in order to preserve a fragile independence.
However, they were never able, like the Swiss, to deter foreign
aggression by demonstrating to the would-be invader that
the venture would prove unacceptably costly. Eventually they
did become the hoped-for ideal—the buffer state—in which

a collection of foreign powers was enlisted to preserve a neutral Laos, as happened at the Geneva conferences of 1954 and 1961–1962.

Such an arrangement was obviously workable only so long as a neutral Laos continued to be in the interests of the parties to the agreement. Once this was no longer so, intervention by foreign states began anew, making Laos a battlefield instead of a buffer state; the big-power guarantees of neutrality were basically unenforceable, despite repeated attempts by Eden, V. M. Molotov, and Chou En-lai after 1954, and by Kennedy and Khrushchev in 1961.

The treatment accorded the three-nation ICSC by the royal government and the Pathet Lao after 1954 is indicative of Laos's future thereafter. True, there were fears, especially by the Chinese, that Laos would sign a mutual security treaty with the United States and become a U.S. military base. But the Laotian group that obstructed the ICSC from carrying out its inspection mission in the hills of Sam Neua was the Pathet Lao. Thus, the Vietnamese "volunteers" were never withdrawn and their presence at the side of the Pathet Lao marked the origin of the first secret war in Laos.

Considering that it had to contend with rightists who championed a military solution to the Pathet Lao problem, the royal government made sincere, even idealistic, attempts to negotiate a political end to the conflict in 1957, in 1962, and finally in 1973. However, the demands in the NLHS platform for peace, independence, and neutrality for Laos were purely tactical. The demand for peace rang hollow in view of the unceasing expansion of the liberated zone by Pathet Lao and North Vietnamese arms, and this neutrality had nothing to do with even-handed relations with Thailand and Vietnam, but existed for the exclusive benefit of North Vietnam, which was steadfastly exempted from the demand that foreign troops quit Laos.

How are we to explain Hanoi's cynical policy toward Laos? There was, admittedly, the precedent set by the French, who, to buttress their colonial empire in Vietnam, resurrected the claims of the Vietnamese emperors to the historic allegiance of the lands beyond the mountains. One is tempted to say that this policy stemmed from Hanoi's strategic need for the Ho Chi Minh Trail and leave it at that. But even before the trail was extended by the North Vietnamese deep into Laotian territory to accommodate Hanoi's escalation of the war in South Vietnam, Hanoi was fostering the "central organ" of the Laotian revolution in the mountains of Sam Neua.

The royal government's attempts to harmonize relations with Hanoi were brought to naught not by the existence of the trail, but by this other interest. Like a constant theme, this underlying interest runs through the abortive attempt of Souvanna Phouma to settle the border issue in Hanoi in 1956, the alliance period of 1961-1962 in which the second coalition extended not much below the prime minister's office, and right through the voluntary resignation of the third coalition as no longer appropriate to the situation. At the end, even though Souvanna Phouma was prepared to let the North Vietnamese have the trail, they did not go away; they stayed.

The imposition of Communist rule in Laos had little if anything to do with cultural factors. Indeed, these mainly worked against Hanoi, since for many years it was forced to rely on the minority groups inhabiting the Laos-Vietnam border region for what little mass support the Pathet Lao could claim. The tiny group who appeared on the tribune of the U.S. gymnasium in Vientiane on December 1, 1975, to accept the reins of power had a unique claim to their position in the fact that they had faithfully obeyed the Vietnamese Communists and their far-sighted leader, Ho Chi Minh, for thirty years. In the coming years, the sacrifices made by the Vietnamese on behalf of the revolution in Laos were to recur like a litany in their joint statements.

Until 1975, the central organ of the revolution in Laos had remained in Sam Neua and the LPRP had been shrouded in total secrecy, its very existence never officially admitted. The so-called revolution in Laos formed part of the larger, Indochinese revolution, which took place in two stages in various Indochinese territories: first national liberation; second socialism. The territories, like the stages, were carefully phased. The LPRP was not merely an offshoot of the ICP; it was the

ICP under a different form, like the Vietnamese Communist party itself and the Hanoi-supported Communist party in Cambodia.

The distinction between the LPRP and the VCP dates from the decision to split the ICP in 1951. Once the revolution in Laos approached the end of its national liberation stage and the Communist seizure of power seemed assured, the phrase "special relationship" began to be introduced in the public lexicon of the followers of the ICP to describe the relations between Laos and Vietnam. This deliberately ambiguous phrase was intended to convey the idea of the same organic unity in state-state relations as prevailed in party-party relations. The phrase is dynamic, not static, implying that Laos's relations with Vietnam were moving ahead to something new. This implication was fully intended from an early date, as is made clear by the invocation of Ho Chi Minh's ceaseless effort on behalf of such relations.

It is thus no accident that the Vietnamese Communist presence in Laos has grown continuously since 1945, when the scarce means available to Ho's faithful band nevertheless allowed them to launch the first steps of an enterprise that required a generation to reach fruition. The twenty-four-year period from the split in the ICP to the LPRP's takeover of power in Vientiane is only slightly longer than the twenty-one years the ICP needed to mature into an organization capable of monopolizing the nationalist mantle in Vietnam. During the former years, Vietnamese actions in Laos can only properly be explained by this special relationship already inscribed in the future of the ICP. Hanoi had a right to be in Laos by virtue of this relationship, for North Vietnam was not really a foreign country and therefore its troops were not really foreign. Otherwise, it would stand convicted of aggression against a sovereign state by any standard of international law.

What is Laos's future according to the ICP? Once the national liberation stage of the revolution in Laos is completed (including the reabsorption of the right-bank provinces), the states will be joined in an Indochinese union with Hanoi as its capital. At that point, the way will be clear for the reconstitution of the split ICP. This sequence of events has already been followed in South Vietnam, where, during the national liberation stage of the revolution, a separate party existed from 1962 forward—the People's Revolutionary party (PRP). In 1976, after national liberation and the reunification of Vietnam, the PRP was quietly merged with the Vietnamese Workers party, whose name was simultaneously changed to Vietnamese Communist party. The LPRP will follow the same path, and the VCP will change its name once more to ICP.

Although unforeseen events may possibly derail this master plan for Indochina, the Vietnamese, sticklers for orderliness, may be expected to resist any attempt at interference (which is not likely). We have only to look at how the Vietnamese reacted in Cambodia, also scheduled to undergo integration into the new Indochina. There, the leaders of Democratic Kampuchea who emerged in October 1976 from the internal struggle for power—Pol Pot, Ieng Sary, Khieu Samphan, Son Sen, and Vorn Vet—were not formed in the ICP tradition. The VCP did not hesitate to crush them by an overt invasion and to replace them with its own people, but not before the Pol Pot faction had liquidated thousands of Hanoi's Cambodian cadres.

Laos's survival, therefore, must be seen in the context of this view of the future held by the Indochinese Communist leaders, including Kaysone and the other LPRP leaders. The takeover in question will not be by outsiders, but rather from within. The Laotians themselves, in another exercise of "democracy," will vote to integrate their country with Vietnam and Cambodia. Then the Indochinese states will form a union similar to the USSR.

As in Eastern Europe, any popular uprising in Vientiane would be quickly crushed by Vietnamese troops. How many tribal revolts will have to be put down to pacify the country? The regime's propaganda is constantly full of references to the threat posed by the schemes of the reactionaries, and Vietnamese repression would easily be justified by invoking the mutual security treaty. Ultimately, however, the traces of nationalistic feeling in Laos will become a matter for the interior ministry to deal with, as they are today for the Estonians, who have been part of the USSR since 1940.

Let us suppose that Laos can survive as a satellite in the same sense that Poland, Czechoslovakia, and the other nations of Eastern Europe survive in the shadow of the USSR without being physically absorbed into the Soviet state. The LPRP, which claims to be leading Laos to socialism, must take into account that Theravada Buddhism is deeply rooted in its traditions. Unless the party intends to enforce a policy of coercion (and there is no firm evidence of this), Buddhism is likely to coexist with the official dogma of Marxism-Leninism for the foreseeable future, as Catholicism does in Poland today.

Such a situation would postpone for some time the final resolution of the national question, and thus the reconstitution of the ICP. During this time, a younger generation of party leaders will have grown up on both sides of the Annamite Chain. Will carrying out Ho Chi Minh's dream of unifying Indochina seem quite so important to them as it does to the present leaders in Hanoi? Will the continued militarization of the region and tensions fed by endless perceived threats, schemes, and border conflicts be accepted? For a generation now, the people of Laos have thirsted for peace: They will undoubtedly accord a greater measure of confidence to rulers who create a credible prospect of bringing it to them.

Selected Bibliography

This note is intended to provide the general reader with references to readily accessible materials on Laos in English.

The standard work of history is D.G.E. Hall's *A History of South-East Asia*, 4th ed. (New York: St. Martin's Press, 1981). This book may usefully be supplemented by H. M. Wright's translation of George Coedès's *Les Peuples de la Péninsule Indochinoise*, under the title *The Making of South East Asia* (Berkeley: University of California Press, reissued 1983). A source article on several aspects of the ancient history of Laos is Lawrence Palmer Briggs's "The Appearance and Historical Usage of the Terms Tai, Thai, Siamese and Lao," *Journal of the American Oriental Society* (Baltimore) 69, no. 2 (April-June 1949):60–73.

Two books describing explorations in Laos are Henri Mouhot's *Diary: Travels in the Central Parts of Siam, Cambodia, and Laos during the Years 1858–61*, abridged and edited by Christopher Pym (New York: Oxford University Press, 1966), and Milton E. Osborne's *River Road to China: The Mekong River Expedition, 1866–1873* (New York: Liveright, 1975).

The most valuable accounts of the dramatic events of 1945–1946 come from interviews with many of the participants, footnoted in Arthur J. Dommen's *Conflict in Laos: The Politics of Neutralization*, rev. ed. (New York: Praeger, 1971) and in Hugh Toye's *Laos: Buffer State or Battleground* (New York: Oxford University Press, 1968), which also contain good bibliographies of the extensive French literature on early Laos. Among those whose memoirs are available in English are Prince Phetsarath (*Iron Man of Laos: Prince Phetsarath Ratanavongsa*, translated by John B. Murdoch and edited by David K. Wyatt, Cornell Southeast Asia Program Data Paper no. 110 [Ithaca, N.Y.: 1978]) and Oun Sananikone (*Lao Issara, The Memoirs of Oun Sananikone*, translated by John B. Murdoch and edited by David K. Wyatt, Cornell Southeast Asia Program Data Paper no. 100 [Ithaca, N.Y.: 1975]). Wyatt's article "Siam and Laos, 1767–1827," *Journal of Southeast Asian History* 4, no. 2 (September 1963):12–32, is also useful.

The U.S. State Department's *Foreign Relations of the United States* series covers up to 1952–1954 (vol. 13, *Indochina*, in two parts [Washington, D.C.: Government Printing Office, 1982]; vol. 16, *The Geneva Conference* [Washington, D.C.: Government Printing Office, 1981]). An excellent account of the 1954 Geneva Conference is given in Robert F. Randle's *Geneva 1954: The Settlement of the Indochinese War* (Princeton, N.J.: Princeton University Press, 1969).

The ICSC reports on implementation of the 1954 Geneva Agreement on Laos are indexed in Dommen's *Conflict in Laos*. A revealing memoir of the crucial 1961–1963 period by the Polish commissioner to the ICSC is Marek Thee's *Notes of a Witness: Laos and the Second Indochinese War* (New York: Random House, 1973).

The various editions of the Pentagon Papers contain much material on Laos, and we are now fortunate in having a translation of the closest thing to Hanoi's "Pentagon Papers" (cited in the text in its Vietnamese edition), *The Anti-U.S. Resistance War for National Salvation 1954–1975: Military Events*, by the War Experiences Recapitulation Committee of the High-Level Military Institute, People's Army Publishing House, Hanoi, 1980 (Arlington, Va.: Joint Publications Research Service, JPRS 80968, 2 June 1982). A Lao memoir that throws light on the military perspective is Major General Oudone Sananikone's *The Royal Lao Army and U.S. Army Advice and Support* (Washington, D.C.: U.S. Army Center of Military History, 1983). A U.S. Navy pilot who survived being shot down and captured in Laos has related his story in Dieter Dengler's *Escape from Laos* (Novata, Calif.: Presidio Press, 1979).

The standard work on the Pathet Lao is Paul F. Langer and Joseph J. Zasloff's *North Vietnam and the Pathet Lao* (Cambridge: Harvard University Press, 1970). First-hand source material includes Kaysone Phomvihane's *Revolution in Laos* (Moscow: Progress Publishers, 1981).

Two books that treat a variety of subjects are *Laos: War and Revolution*, edited by Nina S. Adams and Alfred W. McCoy (New York: Harper & Row, 1970), and *Contemporary Laos: Studies in the Politics and Society of the Lao People's Democratic Republic*, edited by Martin Stuart-Fox (St. Lucia, Australia: University of Queensland Press, 1982).

Those interested in keeping up with current events can do no better than to read the articles in such journals as *Asian Survey* and *Current History*. For more specialized treatment of the Lao Communist party, readers should consult the country articles in *The Yearbook on International Communist Affairs* (Stanford, Calif.: Hoover Institution Press).

Index

173